Delicious Vegetarian Pasta Dishes - Nourishing and Yummy

Emilie A. Franks

All rights reserved.

Copyright © 2024 Emilie A. Franks

Delicious Vegetarian Pasta Dishes - Nourishing and Yummy : Delectable Meatless Pasta Creations - Wholesome and Mouthwatering

Funny helpful tips:

Stay connected with industry peers; collaborations can offer mutual benefits.

Your story is a beacon; share it with pride, inspiring others along the way.

Vegetarian Pasta Recipes So You Can Eat Your Veggies

Shona .J Zamora

All rights reserved. Copyright © 2024 Shona .J Zamora

COPYRIGHT © 2024 Shona .J Zamora

All rights reserved.

No part of this book must be reproduced, stored in a retrieval system, or shared by any means, electronic, mechanical, photocopying, recording, or otherwise, without written permission from the publisher.

Every precaution has been taken in the preparation of this book; still the publisher and author assume no responsibility for errors or omissions. Nor do they assume any liability for damages resulting from the use of the information contained herein.

Legal Notice:

This book is copyright protected and is only meant for your individual use. You are not allowed to amend, distribute, sell, use, quote or paraphrase any of its part without the written consent of the author or publisher.

Introduction

This book invites you on a culinary journey through 300 days of delectable vegetarian pasta recipes. From classic Italian dishes to inventive twists on traditional favorites, this cookbook offers a diverse array of pasta dishes to suit every taste and occasion.

Delight your taste buds with the rich flavors of Mushroom Carbonara, a dish that combines earthy mushrooms with creamy sauce and al dente pasta. Or savor the layers of flavor in the 3-Cheese Eggplant Lasagna, where tender eggplant meets gooey cheese and savory marinara sauce.

For a taste of Italy, try the Absolutely Fabulous Portobello Mushroom Tortellini, a dish that celebrates the earthy richness of portobello mushrooms in delicate pasta pockets. Or indulge in the comforting warmth of Alfredo Blue, a creamy pasta dish that pairs perfectly with a glass of your favorite wine.

Explore the vibrant flavors of Asian cuisine with dishes like Asian Vegan Tofu Noodles, featuring tender tofu and crisp vegetables in a savory sauce. Or enjoy the refreshing simplicity of Avocado Pasta, where ripe avocados add a creamy texture to al dente noodles.

Discover the joy of baking pasta with recipes like Baked Gnocchi With Tomato and Basil, a hearty dish that's perfect for sharing with family and friends. Or try the Baked Macaroni and Cheese, a timeless favorite that's sure to please even the pickiest eaters.

For a taste of the Mediterranean, whip up dishes like the Mediterranean Pasta with Greens, a colorful blend of fresh vegetables and aromatic herbs. Or indulge in the richness of Mushroom and Spinach Ravioli with Chive Butter Sauce, a dish that's as elegant as it is delicious.

Whether you're cooking for a crowd or enjoying a cozy meal for two, this book offers something for everyone. With easy-to-follow recipes and simple ingredients, you'll be whipping up gourmet pasta dishes in no time. So grab your apron and get ready to embark on a culinary adventure that's sure to satisfy your appetite and delight your senses. Happy cooking!

Contents

1. 10 Minute MushroomCarbonara 1
   Ingredients 1
   Direction 1
   Nutrition Information 2
2. 3Cheese Eggplant Lasagna 3
   Ingredients 3
   Direction 4
   Nutrition Information 5
3. Absolutely Fabulous Portobello MushroomTortellini 6
   Ingredients 6
   Direction 7
   Nutrition Information 7
4. Alfredo Blue 8
   Ingredients 8
   Direction 8
   Nutrition Information 9
5. Alfredo Mostaccioli 10
   Ingredients 10
   Direction 10
   Nutrition Information 10
6. Als Quick VegetarianSpaghetti 12
   Ingredients 12
   Direction 12
   Nutrition Information 12
7. Angel Hair Pasta with Pignoli 14
   Ingredients 14
   Direction 14
   Nutrition Information 14
8. Angels Pasta 16
   Ingredients 16

Direction 16
Nutrition Information 16
9. Artichoke Spinach Lasagna 18
Ingredients 18
Direction 18
Nutrition Information 19
10. Asian Vegan Tofu Noodles 20
Ingredients 20
Direction 20
Nutrition Information 21
11. Asparagus Portobello Pasta 22
Ingredients 22
Direction 22
Nutrition Information 23
12. Avocado Pasta 24
Ingredients 24
Direction 24
Nutrition Information 25
13. Awesome Eggplant Pasta 26
Ingredients 26
Direction 26
Nutrition Information 27
14. Baked Gnocchi With Tomato and Basil 28
Ingredients 28
Direction 28
Nutrition Information 29
15. Baked Macaroni and Cheese 30
Ingredients 30
Direction 30
Nutrition Information 31
16. Baked Macaroni and Cheese with Tomato 32
Ingredients 32
Direction 32

Nutrition Information 32
17. Baked Shells in Sauce 34
Ingredients 34
Direction 34
Nutrition Information 34
18. Balsamic Vinegar Tofu and Asparagus Pasta Salad 36
Ingredients 36
Direction 36
Nutrition Information 37
19. Black Bean Lasagna II 38
Ingredients 38
Direction 38
Nutrition Information 39
20. Bleu Cheese Macaroni 40
Ingredients 40
Direction 40
Nutrition Information 41
21. Bow Tie Medley 42
Ingredients 42
Direction 42
Nutrition Information 43
22. Broccoli Lasagna 44
Ingredients 44
Direction 44
Nutrition Information 45
23. Broccoli with Rigatoni 46
Ingredients 46
Direction 46
Nutrition Information 46
24. Broth Pesto with Pasta Peas and Chicken 48
Ingredients 48
Direction 48
Nutrition Information 49

25. Cajun Pasta Fresca	50
Ingredients	50
Direction	50
Nutrition Information	51
26. Carries Artichoke and SunDried Tomato Pasta	52
Ingredients	52
Direction	52
Nutrition Information	53
27. Cathis Florentine Zucchini	54
Ingredients	54
Direction	54
Nutrition Information	55
28. Cheese Lasagna	56
Ingredients	56
Direction	56
Nutrition Information	57
29. Cheesy One Pan Mac AndCheese from Barilla	58
Ingredients	58
Direction	58
Nutrition Information	59
30. Cheesy Spinach Casserole	60
Ingredients	60
Direction	60
Nutrition Information	61
31. Cheesy Vegetable Lasagna	62
Ingredients	62
Direction	62
Nutrition Information	63
32. Cherry Tomato Sauce withPenne	64
Ingredients	64
Direction	64
Nutrition Information	65
33. Cheryls Spinach Cheesy PastaCasserole	66

Ingredients 66
Direction 66
Nutrition Information 67
34. Chickn Parmesan Casserole 68
Ingredients 68
Direction 68
Nutrition Information 69
35. Chucks Favorite Mac and Cheese 70
Ingredients 70
Direction 70
Nutrition Information 71
36. Convenient Vegetarian Lasagna 72
Ingredients 72
Direction 72
Nutrition Information 73
37. Corny Spaghetti 74
Ingredients 74
Direction 74
Nutrition Information 75
38. Couscous Gourmet 76
Ingredients 76
Direction 76
Nutrition Information 77
39. Couscous with Mushrooms and SunDried Tomatoes 78
Ingredients 78
Direction 78
Nutrition Information 79
40. Couscous with Olives and SunDried Tomato 80
Ingredients 80
Direction 80
Nutrition Information 81
41. Cranberry Butternut Squash Couscous 82
Ingredients 82

Direction 82
Nutrition Information 83
42. Creamy Artichoke Pasta 84
Ingredients 84
Direction 84
Nutrition Information 85
43. Creamy Asparagus Pasta 86
Ingredients 86
Direction 86
Nutrition Information 86
44. Creamy Coconut CarbonaraWithout Milk 88
Ingredients 88
Direction 88
Nutrition Information 89
45. Creamy Gorgonzola SpinachPasta 90
Ingredients 90
Direction 90
Nutrition Information 91
46. Creamy Pasta Bake with Cherry Tomatoes and Basil 92
Ingredients 92
Direction 92
Nutrition Information 93
47. Creamy Spinach Tortellini 94
Ingredients 94
Direction 94
Nutrition Information 94
48. Creamy SunDried TomatoCouscous 96
Ingredients 96
Direction 96
Nutrition Information 97
49. Creamy Zucchini withLinguine 98
Ingredients 98
Direction 98

Nutrition Information 99
50. Crispy Chinese Noodles with Eggplant and Peanuts 100
Ingredients 100
Direction 100
Nutrition Information 101
51. Curried Couscous with Spinach and Chickpeas 103
Ingredients 103
Direction 103
Nutrition Information 104
52. Debbies Vegetable Lasagna 105
Ingredients 105
Direction 105
Nutrition Information 106
53. Delicious Angel Hair Pasta 107
Ingredients 107
Direction 107
Nutrition Information 108
54. Easy Fettucine Alfredo 109
Ingredients 109
Direction 109
Nutrition Information 109
55. Easy Pasta Bake with Leek and Cheese 111
Ingredients 111
Direction 111
Nutrition Information 112
56. Easy Roasted Vegetable Lasagna 113
Ingredients 113
Direction 113
Nutrition Information 114
57. Easy Spinach Lasagna with White Sauce 115
Ingredients 115
Direction 115
Nutrition Information 116

58. Easy Vegan Pasta with Kaleand Chickpeas 117
Ingredients 117
Direction 117
Nutrition Information 118
59. Easy Vegetarian Red BeansLasagna 119
Ingredients 119
Direction 119
Nutrition Information 120
60. Easy Vegetarian Spaghettiwith Zucchini Tomato andFeta 121
Ingredients 121
Direction 121
Nutrition Information 122
61. Easy Vegetarian SpinachLasagna 123
Ingredients 123
Direction 123
Nutrition Information 124
62. Easy Vegetarian Stroganoff 125
Ingredients 125
Direction 125
Nutrition Information 125
63. Eggplant Pasta 127
Ingredients 127
Direction 127
Nutrition Information 127
64. Eggplant Pasta Bake 129
Ingredients 129
Direction 129
Nutrition Information 130
65. Fabulous Cilantro Pesto 131
Ingredients 131
Direction 131
Nutrition Information 132
66. Farfalle Pasta with Zucchiniand LemonCream Sauce 133

Ingredients 133
Direction 133
Nutrition Information 134
67.   Fettuccine Alfredo III 135
Ingredients 135
Direction 135
Nutrition Information 135
68.   Fettuccine in Creamy Mushroom and Sage Sauce 137
Ingredients 137
Direction 137
Nutrition Information 137
69.   Fettuccine Pasta withPortobello Mushrooms 139
Ingredients 139
Direction 139
Nutrition Information 140
70.   Fettuccini al Fungi 141
Ingredients 141
Direction 141
Nutrition Information 141
71.   Fire and Ice Pasta 143
Ingredients 143
Direction 143
Nutrition Information 144
72.   FireRoasted Tomato andSpinach Pasta 145
Ingredients 145
Direction 145
Nutrition Information 146
73.   Flashblasted Broccoli andFeta Pasta 147
Ingredients 147
Direction 147
Nutrition Information 148
74.   Four Cheese Macaroni andCheese 149
Ingredients 149

Direction 149
Nutrition Information 150
75. Four Cheese Macaroni Casserole 151
Ingredients 151
Direction 151
Nutrition Information 152
76. Fresh Tomato Pasta 153
Ingredients 153
Direction 153
Nutrition Information 153
77. Fusilli with Rapini Broccoli Rabe Garlic and Tomato Wine Sauce 155
Ingredients 155
Direction 155
Nutrition Information 156
78. Game Day Mac and Mex 157
Ingredients 157
Direction 157
Nutrition Information 158
79. Garage Noodles 159
Ingredients 159
Direction 159
Nutrition Information 159
80. Garlicky Vodka Alfredo 161
Ingredients 161
Direction 161
Nutrition Information 162
81. Ginas Creamy Mushroom Lasagna 163
Ingredients 163
Direction 163
Nutrition Information 165
82. Gnocchi and Peppers in Balsamic Sauce 166
Ingredients 166
Direction 166

Nutrition Information 167
83. Gnocchi I 168
Ingredients 168
Direction 168
Nutrition Information 168
84. Gnocchi Primavera 170
Ingredients 170
Direction 170
Nutrition Information 171
85. Gorgonzola Cream Sauce 172
Ingredients 172
Direction 172
Nutrition Information 173
86. Grandmas Gnocchi 174
Ingredients 174
Direction 174
Nutrition Information 174
87. Greek Fettuccine 176
Ingredients 176
Direction 176
Nutrition Information 176
88. Greek God Pasta 178
Ingredients 178
Direction 178
Nutrition Information 179
89. Greek Orzo with Feta 180
Ingredients 180
Direction 180
Nutrition Information 180
90. Greek Pasta with Tomatoesand White Beans 182
Ingredients 182
Direction 182
Nutrition Information 182

91. Greek Spaghetti II	184
Ingredients	184
Direction	184
Nutrition Information	184
92. Green Green Pasta	186
Ingredients	186
Direction	186
Nutrition Information	187
93. Hearty Vegetable Lasagna	188
Ingredients	188
Direction	188
Nutrition Information	189
94. Homemade Four CheeseRavioli	190
Ingredients	190
Direction	191
Nutrition Information	192
95. Homemade GlutenFree andLactoseFree Vegetable Lasagna	193
Ingredients	193
Direction	194
Nutrition Information	194
96. Homemade Mac and Cheese	196
Ingredients	196
Direction	196
Nutrition Information	197
97. Homestyle Mushroom Lasagna	198
Ingredients	198
Direction	198
Nutrition Information	199
98. Hot Tomato Sauce	200
Ingredients	200
Direction	200
Nutrition Information	200
99. Italian Veggie Rolls	202

Ingredients 202
Direction 202
Nutrition Information 203
100. Jajangmyeon Vegetarian Korean Black Bean Noodles 204
Ingredients 204
Direction 204
Nutrition Information 205
101. KaesSpaetzle 206
Ingredients 206
Direction 206
Nutrition Information 207
102. Kicked Up Mac and Cheese 208
Ingredients 208
Direction 208
Nutrition Information 209
103. Lasagna Roll Ups 210
Ingredients 210
Direction 210
Nutrition Information 211
104. Lasagna Spinach RollUps 212
Ingredients 212
Direction 212
Nutrition Information 213
105. Lasagna Spirals 214
Ingredients 214
Direction 214
Nutrition Information 215
106. Lazy Pierogi 216
Ingredients 216
Direction 216
Nutrition Information 216
107. Lemon Coconut ThaiInspiredPasta 218
Ingredients 218

Direction	218
Nutrition Information	219
108. Lemon Parmesan Spaghetti	220
Ingredients	220
Direction	220
Nutrition Information	221
109. Linguine with PortobelloMushrooms	222
Ingredients	222
Direction	222
Nutrition Information	223
110. Linguini with Vegetables	224
Ingredients	224
Direction	224
Nutrition Information	225
111. Lo Mein Noodles	226
Ingredients	226
Direction	226
Nutrition Information	227
112. Lovely Linguine	228
Ingredients	228
Direction	228
Nutrition Information	228
113. Low Fat Cheesy Spinach andEggplant Lasagna	230
Ingredients	230
Direction	230
Nutrition Information	231
114. LowCalorie Vegetarian FilipinoPancit	232
Ingredients	232
Direction	232
Nutrition Information	233
115. Lucys Mac and Corn	234
Ingredients	234
Direction	234

Nutrition Information	234
116. Mac and Cheese II	236
Ingredients	236
Direction	236
Nutrition Information	236
117. Mac and Shews Vegan Macand Cheese	238
Ingredients	238
Direction	238
Nutrition Information	239
118. Macaroni and Cheese III	240
Ingredients	240
Direction	240
Nutrition Information	241
119. Macaroni and Cheese V	242
Ingredients	242
Direction	242
Nutrition Information	243
120. Manicotti	244
Ingredients	244
Direction	244
Nutrition Information	245
121. Manicotti Pancakes I	246
Ingredients	246
Direction	246
Nutrition Information	246
122. Manicotti Pancakes II	248
Ingredients	248
Direction	248
Nutrition Information	248
123. MeatFree Stuffed Shells	249
Ingredients	249
Direction	249
Nutrition Information	250

124. Meatless Eggplant Lasagna	251
Ingredients	251
Direction	251
Nutrition Information	252
125. Mediterranean Pasta withGreens	253
Ingredients	253
Direction	253
Nutrition Information	254
126. Mediterranean Whole WheatPasta Toss	255
Ingredients	255
Direction	255
Nutrition Information	256
127. MediterraneanStyle EggplantPasta	257
Ingredients	257
Direction	257
Nutrition Information	258
128. Michelles Vegan Lasagna	259
Ingredients	259
Direction	260
Nutrition Information	260
129. Moms Baked Macaroni andCheese	261
Ingredients	261
Direction	261
Nutrition Information	261
130. Moms Favorite Baked Mac andCheese	262
Ingredients	262
Direction	262
Nutrition Information	263
131. Moms Macaroni and Cheese	264
Ingredients	264
Direction	264
Nutrition Information	265
132. Moms Peas and Noodles	266

Ingredients 266
Direction 266
Nutrition Information 266
133. Monterey Spaghetti 268
Ingredients 268
Direction 268
Nutrition Information 269
134. Mostaccioli with Spinach andFeta 270
Ingredients 270
Direction 270
Nutrition Information 270
135. Mushroom and Spinach Ravioliwith Chive Butter Sauce 272
Ingredients 272
Direction 273
Nutrition Information 274
136. Mushroom Kale and Bok ChoyRamen 275
Ingredients 275
Direction 275
Nutrition Information 276
137. Mushroom Spinach Mac andCheese 277
Ingredients 277
Direction 277
Nutrition Information 278
138. NoCream Pasta Primavera 279
Ingredients 279
Direction 280
Nutrition Information 280
139. Old Fashioned Mac andCheese 281
Ingredients 281
Direction 281
Nutrition Information 282
140. Olive and Feta Pasta 283
Ingredients 283

Direction 283
Nutrition Information 283
141. Orzo and Potato Parmesan 285
Ingredients 285
Direction 285
Nutrition Information 286
142. Orzo with SunDried Tomatoesand Kalamata Olives 287
Ingredients 287
Direction 287
Nutrition Information 287
143. Oyster Mushroom Pasta 289
Ingredients 289
Direction 289
Nutrition Information 290
144. Pad Thai 291
Ingredients 291
Direction 291
Nutrition Information 292
145. Pad Thai with Tofu 293
Ingredients 293
Direction 293
Nutrition Information 294
146. Pasta and Bean Casserole 295
Ingredients 295
Direction 295
Nutrition Information 296
147. Pasta and Vegetable Saute 297
Ingredients 297
Direction 297
Nutrition Information 298
148. Pasta and White Beans Gratin 299
Ingredients 299
Direction 299

Nutrition Information 300
149. Pasta Carcione 301
Ingredients 301
Direction 301
Nutrition Information 301
150. Pasta Pascal 303
Ingredients 303
Direction 303
Nutrition Information 303
151. Pasta Shells Florentine 305
Ingredients 305
Direction 305
Nutrition Information 306
152. Pasta Shells with Portobello Mushrooms and Asparagus inBoursin Sauce ... 307
Ingredients 307
Direction 307
Nutrition Information 308
153. Pasta Siciliano 309
Ingredients 309
Direction 309
Nutrition Information 309
154. Pasta with Arugula andTomatoes 311
Ingredients 311
Direction 311
Nutrition Information 312
155. Pasta with Arugula Pesto 313
Ingredients 313
Direction 313
Nutrition Information 314
156. Pasta with Asparagus andLemon Sauce 315
Ingredients 315
Direction 315
Nutrition Information 316

157. Pasta with Asparagus GoatCheese and Lemon 317
Ingredients 317
Direction 317
Nutrition Information 318
158. Pasta with Baby Broccoli andBeans 319
Ingredients 319
Direction 319
Nutrition Information 320
159. Pasta with Cilantro Pesto andBarley 321
Ingredients 321
Direction 321
Nutrition Information 322
160. Pasta with Fresh TomatoSauce 323
Ingredients 323
Direction 323
Nutrition Information 323

1. # 10 Minute Mushroom Carbonara

"This is a quick and easy upgrade to weeknight spaghetti dinner. I tend to make this low sodium, but you may want to add salt in the pasta water and while the mushrooms are cooking."

Serving: 6 | Prep: 5 m | Cook: 12 m | Ready in: 17 m

Ingredients

- 1 (16 ounce) package spaghetti

- 1/2 pound sliced fresh mushrooms
- 1 tablespoon olive oil
- 2 cloves garlic
- 3 eggs
- 1/2 cup freshly grated Parmesan cheese divided

Direction

- Bring a large pot of lightly salted water to a boil. Cook spaghetti in the boiling water, stirring occasionally, until tender yet firm to the bite, about 12 minutes. Drain.
- Meanwhile, place mushrooms in a dry skillet over medium heat. Cook until they begin to brown and release moisture, 3 to 5 minutes. Add oil and garlic. Fry until softened, about 3 minutes more.
- Beat eggs together in a bowl. Add 1/2 the Parmesan cheese. Mix well and stir into cooked mushroom mixture.
- Serve the pasta topped with mushroom sauce and remaining Parmesan cheese.

Nutrition Information

- Calories: 371 calories
- Total Fat: 7.9 g
- Cholesterol: 99 mg
- Sodium: 144 mg
- Total Carbohydrate: 57.8 g
- Protein: 16.7 g

2. 3Cheese Eggplant Lasagna

"This recipe is chock full of great vegetables. Measurements of spices vary according to our taste; you should always adjust recipes to your own preferences!"

Serving: 8 | Prep: 40 m | Cook: 45 m | Ready in: 2 h 25 m

Ingredients

- 2 eggplants, sliced lengthwise into 1/4-inch thick slices
- 2 tablespoons salt
- 2 tablespoons canola oil
- 1 (28 ounce) can crushed tomatoes
- 1 (6 ounce) can tomato paste
- 1 teaspoon dried oregano
- 1 teaspoon dried basil
- 1 teaspoon garlic powder
- 1 teaspoon onion powder
- 1 tablespoon olive oil
- salt and ground black pepper to taste
- 1 teaspoon olive oil
- 1 onion, diced
- 1 cup frozen chopped spinach

- 1 cup shredded carrot
- 1 (15 ounce) container ricotta cheese
- 2 eggs
- 1/2 cup freshly grated Romano cheese
- 1 teaspoon garlic powder
- 1 teaspoon onion powder
- 1/2 teaspoon salt
- 1 cup shredded mozzarella cheese

Direction

- Sprinkle both sides of eggplant slices with 2 tablespoons salt, and layer them in a large baking dish with paper towels between each layer.
- Place a smaller baking dish on top of the eggplant slices, and weigh it down with several heavy food cans. Let sit for at least an hour or until the paper towels are visibly moist.
- Rinse eggplant slices with fresh water and pat dry with paper towels.
- Heat a large skillet on medium heat and pour in 2 tablespoons of canola oil.
- Working in batches if necessary, cook both sides of eggplant slices until they are slightly browned, about 5 minutes per side. Set cooked eggplant aside.
- Prepare sauce by combining the crushed tomatoes, tomato paste, oregano, basil, 1 teaspoon garlic powder, 1 teaspoon onion powder, 1 tablespoon olive oil, salt, and black pepper in a separate bowl. Set aside.
- Heat 1 teaspoon olive oil in a skillet over medium heat; cook and stir onion until translucent, about 5 minutes.
- Add frozen spinach and shredded carrots to onion. Cook until mixture is dry, 5 to 8 minutes. Set aside to cool.

- Combine ricotta cheese, eggs, Romano cheese, 1 teaspoon garlic powder, 1 teaspoon onion powder, and 1/2 teaspoon salt in a separate bowl.
- Spoon cooled spinach and carrot mixture into ricotta mixture and combine.
- Preheat oven to 350 degrees F (175 degrees C).
- Begin lasagna assembly by pouring a thin layer of tomato sauce into a 9x13 inch baking dish.
- Place half the eggplant slices in a layer on top of tomato sauce.
- Spread half the ricotta cheese mixture on top of eggplant layer.
- Add another layer of tomato sauce, then layer on the remaining eggplant slices and remaining ricotta mixture.
- Finish with a final layer of tomato sauce, and spread mozzarella cheese over the top.
- Bake in the preheated oven for 45 minutes or until the mozzarella cheese is browned. Let sit for 10 minutes before serving.

Nutrition Information

- Calories: 285 calories
- Total Fat: 16 g
- Cholesterol: 80 mg
- Sodium: 2475 mg
- Total Carbohydrate: 20.8 g
- Protein: 17.3 g

3. Absolutely Fabulous Portobello Mushroom Tortellini

"Gourmet, delicious, and so easy - what could be better? A must for impromptu dinner guests."

Serving: 4 | Prep: 10 m | Cook: 15 m | Ready in: 25 m

Ingredients

- 1 pound cheese tortellini
- 2 large portobello mushrooms
- 1/4 cup white wine
- 1 tablespoon chopped fresh parsley
- 2 cloves garlic, minced
- 8 ounces Alfredo-style pasta sauce
- salt and pepper to taste
- 1/3 cup grated Parmesan cheese

Direction

- Bring a large pot of lightly salted water to a boil. Add pasta and cook for 8 to 10 minutes or until al dente; drain.
- Meanwhile, prepare mushrooms by rinsing and thinly slicing the mushroom caps; discard the stems.
- In a medium skillet over low heat, combine wine, parsley, garlic and mushrooms; stirring frequently, sauté for approximately 5 minutes or until mushrooms are cooked through.
- Remove skillet from heat and slowly add Alfredo sauce, stirring to blend; season with salt and pepper to taste.
- Separate hot pasta into four portions and spoon sauce over pasta. Garnish with cheese and serve immediately.

Nutrition Information

- Calories: 470 calories
- Total Fat: 25.4 g
- Cholesterol: 55 mg
- Sodium: 933 mg
- Total Carbohydrate: 42.2 g
- Protein: 18.3 g

4. Alfredo Blue

"This is the best alfredo sauce I have ever come up with and any kind of meat or vegetable can be added to it."

Serving: 8 | Prep: 10 m | Cook: 25 m | Ready in: 35 m

Ingredients

- 1 (16 ounce) package fettuccini pasta
- 1 tablespoon olive oil
- 1 clove garlic, sliced
- 4 ounces blue cheese, crumbled
- 1/4 cup grated Parmesan cheese
- 2 cups heavy cream
- 1 tablespoon Italian seasoning
- salt and pepper to taste

Direction

- Bring a large pot of lightly salted water to a boil. Cook pasta in boiling water for 8 to 10 minutes, or until al dente; drain.
- Heat olive oil in a small skillet over medium heat. Sauté garlic in olive oil until golden. Remove garlic, and reserve oil.
- In a medium saucepan over medium-low heat, combine blue cheese, Parmesan cheese, and cream. Stir until cheeses are melted. Stir in the oil from the garlic pan. Season with Italian seasoning, salt, and pepper.
- Toss sauce with hot pasta, and let stand 5 minutes before serving.

Nutrition Information

- Calories: 487 calories
- Total Fat: 29.9 g
- Cholesterol: 94 mg
- Sodium: 262 mg
- Total Carbohydrate: 43.9 g
- Protein: 12.9 g

5. Alfredo Mostaccioli

"My friends love this Alfredo sauce and it can be used with any type pasta that will hold sauce well. I've also used this as a base for making a white pizza and it is excellent! Enjoy!"

Serving: 8 | Prep: 10 m | Cook: 15 m | Ready in: 25 m

Ingredients

- 1 (16 ounce) package mostaccioli
- 1 cup heavy cream
- 1/2 cup butter
- 1/2 cup grated Parmesan cheese
- 1 cup chopped fresh parsley
- 1 teaspoon salt
- 1/4 teaspoon freshly ground black pepper
- 1/8 teaspoon garlic powder

Direction

- Bring a large pot of lightly salted water to a boil. Add pasta and cook for 8 to 10 minutes or until al dente; drain.
- Combine heavy cream and butter in a Dutch oven or large, heavy saucepan over medium heat. Heat until butter melts, stirring occasionally; be careful not to bring mixture to a boil. Stir in Parmesan cheese, parsley, salt, pepper and garlic powder. Toss with cooked pasta and serve immediately.

Nutrition Information

- Calories: 430 calories

- Total Fat: 25.3 g
- Cholesterol: 76 mg
- Sodium: 467 mg
- Total Carbohydrate: 42.4 g
- Protein: 10.3 g

6. Als Quick Vegetarian Spaghetti

"This is a quick meal to satisfy guests who do not eat meat. It will fill you up. Buy a chunky tomato sauce to make your sauce thicker."

Serving: 8 | Prep: 10 m | Cook: 20 m | Ready in: 30 m

Ingredients

- 1 pound uncooked spaghetti
- 1 cup broccoli florets
- 1 (15 ounce) can whole kernel corn, drained
- 1 cup fresh sliced mushrooms
- 1 cup sliced carrots
- 2 (8 ounce) cans tomato sauce

Direction

- Bring a large pot of salted water to boil, add spaghetti and return water to a boil. Cook until spaghetti is al dente; drain well.
- Combine broccoli, corn, mushrooms, carrots and tomato sauce in large sauce pot. Cook on medium heat for 15 to 20 minutes or until vegetables are tender. Stir occasionally to keep sauce from sticking. Serve sauce over spaghetti.

Nutrition Information

- Calories: 279 calories
- Total Fat: 1.6 g

- Cholesterol: 0 mg
- Sodium: 468 mg
- Total Carbohydrate: 57.8 g
- Protein: 10.3 g

7. Angel Hair Pasta with Pignoli

"Serves 2 as an entree, or 4 as a first course."

Serving: 3

Ingredients

- 3/4 cup pine nuts
- 1/2 cup clarified butter
- 1 1/4 cups heavy whipping cream
- 2 1/3 tablespoons butter
- 1 pinch ground nutmeg
- salt to taste
- 1 pinch freshly ground white pepper
- 1 (8 ounce) package angel hair pasta

Direction

- Toast pignoli nuts slowly in a skillet, watching carefully not to burn. Remove from skillet when nuts are tan in color.
- Cook noodles in boiling salted water until al dente. Drain.
- Combine heavy cream, clarified butter, 2 1/3 tablespoons butter or margarine, nutmeg, and salt and pepper in a saucepan; heat thoroughly. Add noodles to the heated sauce. Let sauce reduce to a creamy consistency. Top with nuts, and serve.

Nutrition Information

- Calories: 1129 calories
- Total Fat: 99 g

- Cholesterol: 247 mg
- Sodium: 257 mg
- Total Carbohydrate: 49.4 g
- Protein: 18.4 g

8. Angels Pasta

"Light and delicate vegetarian pasta entree that's easy!"

Serving: 6 | Prep: 10 m | Cook: 15 m | Ready in: 25 m

Ingredients

- 8 ounces angel hair pasta
- 1 tablespoon crushed garlic
- 1 tablespoon olive oil
- 2 zucchini, sliced
- salt and pepper to taste
- 3 tomatoes, chopped
- 12 leaves fresh basil
- 4 ounces mozzarella cheese, shredded

Direction

- Bring a large pot of lightly salted water to a boil. Add pasta and cook for 8 to 10 minutes or until al dente; drain.
- Meanwhile, heat a medium skillet over medium heat. Pour in oil and sauté garlic until golden. Stir in zucchini, salt and pepper. Sauté 2 minutes, then mix in tomato and cook a few minutes more. Chop basil and add to vegetables right before mixing with pasta.
- Combine pasta and vegetables. Serve topped with mozzarella.

Nutrition Information

- Calories: 201 calories

- Total Fat: 6.6 g
- Cholesterol: 12 mg
- Sodium: 202 mg
- Total Carbohydrate: 26.9 g
- Protein: 10.1 g

9. Artichoke Spinach Lasagna

"This is a fabulous lasagna made with an artichoke and spinach mixture which has been cooked with vegetable broth, onions and garlic. The mixture is layered with lasagna noodles, pasta sauce, mozzarella cheese, and topped with crumbled feta."

Serving: 8 | Prep: 20 m | Cook: 1 h | Ready in: 1 h 20 m

Ingredients

- cooking spray
- 9 uncooked lasagna noodles
- 1 onion, chopped
- 4 cloves garlic, chopped
- 1 (14.5 ounce) can vegetable broth
- 1 tablespoon chopped fresh rosemary
- 1 (14 ounce) can marinated artichoke hearts, drained and chopped
- 1 (10 ounce) package frozen chopped spinach, thawed, drained and squeezed dry
- 1 (28 ounce) jar tomato pasta sauce
- 3 cups shredded mozzarella cheese, divided
- 1 (4 ounce) package herb and garlic feta, crumbled

Direction

- Preheat oven to 350 degrees F (175 degrees C). Spray a 9x13 inch baking dish with cooking spray.
- Bring a large pot of lightly salted water to a boil. Add noodles and cook for 8 to 10 minutes or until al dente; drain.

- Spray a large skillet with cooking spray and heat on medium-high. Sauté onion and garlic for 3 minutes, or until onion is tender-crisp. Stir in broth and rosemary; bring to a boil. Stir in artichoke hearts and spinach; reduce heat, cover and simmer 5 minutes. Stir in pasta sauce.
- Spread 1/4 of the artichoke mixture in the bottom of the prepared baking dish; top with 3 cooked noodles. Sprinkle 3/4 cup mozzarella cheese over noodles. Repeat layers 2 more times, ending with artichoke mixture and mozzarella cheese. Sprinkle crumbled feta on top.
- Bake, covered, for 40 minutes. Uncover, and bake 15 minutes more, or until hot and bubbly. Let stand 10 minutes before cutting.

Nutrition Information

- Calories: 396 calories
- Total Fat: 16 g
- Cholesterol: 42 mg
- Sodium: 1139 mg
- Total Carbohydrate: 44.5 g
- Protein: 21.1 g

10. Asian Vegan Tofu Noodles

"A vegan rice noodle base with marinated tofu and vegetables. I like to also serve it with vegan chili-mayo, but it tastes great without as well."

Serving: 2 | Prep: 25 m | Cook: 15 m | Ready in: 55 m

Ingredients

- 1/4 (16 ounce) package dried rice noodles
- 1/2 (12 ounce) package firm tofu, cubed
- 1/4 cup soy sauce
- 3 tablespoons coconut oil, divided
- 1 teaspoon teriyaki sauce
- 2 cloves garlic, minced, divided
- 1/4 teaspoon cayenne pepper, or to taste
- salt and ground black pepper to taste
- 1 red bell pepper, cubed
- 1/2 cup fresh green beans, cut into 1/2-inch pieces
- 1 teaspoon grated fresh ginger
- sesame seeds, or to taste
- 1/2 teaspoon vegetable seasoning, or to taste
- Sauce:
- 4 tablespoons vegan or eggless mayonnaise
- 1 tablespoon fresh lemon juice, or to taste
- 1 tablespoon Asian red chile sauce, such as Sriracha®, or to taste
- 1 teaspoon cider vinegar
- 1 splash soy sauce
- salt and freshly ground black pepper to taste

Direction

- Place noodles in a large bowl and cover with boiling water. Set aside until noodles are softened, about 15 minutes. Drain and rinse thoroughly.
- Combine tofu, soy sauce, 1 tablespoon coconut oil, teriyaki sauce, 1/2 of the garlic, cayenne pepper, salt, and pepper in a bowl and set aside while preparing the rest of the ingredients.
- Heat remaining 2 tablespoons coconut oil in a large skillet over low heat and cook the remaining garlic until fragrant, about 2 minutes. Add bell pepper and green beans and cook until softened, about 5 minutes. Remove tofu from marinade and add to vegetables. Sprinkle with sesame seeds and mix well. Season with vegetable seasoning, salt, and pepper. Stir-fry for 2 minutes. Cover and cook for 3 minutes. Add drained noodles and stir to combine.
- Combine vegan mayonnaise, lemon juice, red chile sauce, vinegar, soy sauce, salt and pepper in a bowl. Serve with the tofu noodles.

Nutrition Information

- Calories: 528 calories
- Total Fat: 27.2 g
- Cholesterol: 0 mg
- Sodium: 2534 mg
- Total Carbohydrate: 60.4 g
- Protein: 13.1 g

11. Asparagus Portobello Pasta

"Tasty pasta covered in an asparagus based sauce with sauteed portobello mushrooms and peas. "

Serving: 4 | Prep: 10 m | Cook: 20 m | Ready in: 30 m

Ingredients

- 2 (15 ounce) cans asparagus
- 1 (2.25 ounce) can sliced black olives
- 1/2 pound fettuccini pasta
- 1 tablespoon olive oil
- 3 large portobello mushrooms, sliced
- 1 (8 ounce) can peas, drained
- 2 teaspoons Italian seasoning
- 1 (6 ounce) can tomato paste
- 1/2 cup grated Parmesan cheese

Direction

- Fill a large pot with water and the drained liquids of the asparagus and the olives; bring to a boil. Cook pasta for 8 to 10 minutes, or until al dente. Drain.
- Meanwhile, heat oil in a large skillet over medium heat. Sauté mushrooms, peas, and Italian seasoning until mushrooms are tender.
- In a blender or food processor, puree asparagus, black olives, tomato paste and Parmesan. Transfer to a small saucepan, and heat through over medium-low heat. Spoon asparagus sauce over fettuccini, and top with mushrooms and peas.

Nutrition Information

- Calories: 390 calories
- Total Fat: 10.1 g
- Cholesterol: 9 mg
- Sodium: 1248 mg
- Total Carbohydrate: 61.5 g
- Protein: 19.6 g

12. Avocado Pasta

"This avocado pasta recipe is amazing! Fresh garlic livens up some whole grain penne pasta. Fresh herbs add lots of flavor."

Serving: 2 | Prep: 15 m | Cook: 15 m | Ready in: 30 m

Ingredients

- 1/2 (16 ounce) package whole wheat penne
- 2 tablespoons olive oil
- 1 lime, zested and juiced
- 2 tablespoons chopped fresh mint
- 2 tablespoons chopped fresh chives
- 2 cloves garlic, pressed
- 1 tablespoon nutritional yeast (optional)
- salt and freshly ground black pepper to taste
- 1 cup bean sprouts
- 1 avocado - peeled, pitted and sliced

Direction

- Bring a large pot of lightly salted water to a boil; add penne and cook, stirring occasionally, until tender yet firm to the bite, about 10 minutes. Drain and return to pot.
- Whisk olive oil, lime zest and juice, mint, chives, garlic, nutritional yeast, salt, and pepper together in a bowl. Pour over hot pasta; add bean sprouts. Toss to coat.
- Serve topped with avocado slices and more freshly ground black pepper.

Nutrition Information

- Calories: 381 calories
- Total Fat: 15.2 g
- Cholesterol: 0 mg
- Sodium: 84 mg
- Total Carbohydrate: 51.7 g
- Protein: 11.8 g

13. Awesome Eggplant Pasta

"This is a quick week night pasta that is delicious and tastes like you slaved over it! Garnish with fresh basil and serve immediately."

Serving: 6 | Prep: 10 m | Cook: 50 m | Ready in: 1 h

Ingredients

- 2 teaspoons olive oil, divided
- 1 sweet onion, chopped
- 1 (28 ounce) can whole peeled tomatoes
- 10 fresh basil leaves
- 1 eggplant, peeled and cubed
- 1 portobello mushroom, chopped
- 1 red bell pepper, diced
- 1 (16 ounce) package rigatoni pasta
- 1 (8 ounce) package fresh mozzarella cheese, cubed, or to taste

Direction

- Heat 1 teaspoon olive oil in a skillet over medium heat; cook and stir onion until translucent, about 10 minutes. Add tomatoes and fresh basil and bring to a simmer.
- Heat remaining olive oil in a separate skillet over medium heat; cook and stir eggplant, mushroom, and red bell pepper until softened, about 10 minutes. Add tomato mixture to eggplant mixture and simmer for 30 minutes.
- Bring a large pot of lightly salted water to a boil. Cook rigatoni in the boiling water, stirring occasionally until cooked through but firm to the bite, about 13 minutes. Drain.

- Toss pasta, mozzarella cheese, and tomato sauce together in a bowl.

Nutrition Information

- Calories: 460 calories
- Total Fat: 11.9 g
- Cholesterol: 30 mg
- Sodium: 250 mg
- Total Carbohydrate: 71.3 g
- Protein: 19.7 g

14. Baked Gnocchi With Tomato and Basil

"Delicious dish with great flavor due to the browning of the gnocchi which gives it a crisp exterior. A quick tomato sauce is built in the empty skillet. The gnocchi goes back into the sauce and is finished with mozzarella under the broiler."

Serving: 4 | Prep: 10 m | Cook: 25 m | Ready in: 35 m

Ingredients

- 3 tablespoons extra-virgin olive oil, divided
- 1 pound refrigerated gnocchi
- 1 onion, finely chopped
- 6 cloves garlic, minced
- 1/8 teaspoon red pepper flakes
- 1 (28 ounce) can crushed tomatoes
- 1 cup water
- 1/2 cup chopped fresh basil
- 2 cups shredded mozzarella cheese

Direction

- Adjust oven rack to upper-middle position and preheat oven to 475 degrees F (245 degrees C).
- Heat 2 tablespoons oil in a large heatproof nonstick skillet over medium-high heat. Sauté gnocchi until lightly browned, about 4 minutes. Transfer to a plate.
- Heat the remaining oil in the same skillet. Add onion; cook and stir until onion is softened, about 3 minutes. Stir in garlic and red pepper flakes and cook until fragrant, about 30 seconds.

Stir in tomatoes and water; cook until slightly thickened, about 5 minutes.
- Place gnocchi back in the skillet; add basil. Reduce heat to low and simmer, stirring occasionally, until gnocchi is tender, 5 to 7 minutes. Sprinkle mozzarella cheese on top.
- Transfer skillet to the preheated oven. Bake until cheese is well browned, about 8 minutes.

Nutrition Information

- Calories: 490 calories
- Total Fat: 27.7 g
- Cholesterol: 57 mg
- Sodium: 699 mg
- Total Carbohydrate: 42.9 g
- Protein: 20.9 g

15. Baked Macaroni and Cheese

"A friend of mine sent this recipe to me when I got my first apartment, because she knows how much I hate cooking! It's really easy -- even I can make it -- and tastes great. I'm not sure where she found the recipe, but it included the note 'Good source of protein, vitamin A, B group vitamins, calcium.'"

Serving: 3

Ingredients

- 1 (12 ounce) package macaroni
- 1 egg
- 2 cups milk
- 2 tablespoons butter, melted
- 2 1/2 cups shredded Cheddar cheese
- salt and pepper to taste

Direction

- Preheat the oven to 350 degrees F (175 degrees C). Lightly grease a 2-quart baking dish.
- In a large pot of salted water, lightly boil the macaroni for about 5 minutes until half-cooked.
- Whisk the egg and milk together in a large cup. Add butter and cheese to the egg and milk. Stir well.
- Place the lightly cooked macaroni in the prepared baking dish. Pour the egg and cheese liquid over the macaroni, sprinkle with salt and pepper, and stir well. Press the mixture evenly around the baking dish.
- Bake uncovered, for 30 to 40 minutes, or until the top is brown.

Nutrition Information

- Calories: 968 calories
- Total Fat: 45.4 g
- Cholesterol: 194 mg
- Sodium: 736 mg
- Total Carbohydrate: 92.6 g
- Protein: 45.6 g

16. Baked Macaroni and Cheese with Tomato

"This is a quick and easy dinner or lunch recipe that has been in my family for years. Tomato soup adds a twist of flavor."

Serving: 6 | Prep: 30 m | Cook: 45 m | Ready in: 1 h 15 m

Ingredients

- 1 pound macaroni
- 1 (10.75 ounce) can condensed tomato soup
- 1 1/4 cups milk
- 3 cups shredded Cheddar cheese
- 8 tablespoons butter, divided
- 1/4 cup dry bread crumbs

Direction

- Preheat oven to 350 degrees F (175 degrees C). Bring a large pot of lightly salted water to a boil. Pour in pasta and cook for 8 to 10 minutes or until al dente; drain.
- In large bowl, combine macaroni, soup, milk, cheese and 6 tablespoons butter. Pour into 9x13 baking dish. Top with bread crumbs and dot with remaining butter. Bake for 45 minutes or until golden brown and bubbly.

Nutrition Information

- Calories: 740 calories
- Total Fat: 37.9 g

- Cholesterol: 104 mg
- Sodium: 797 mg
- Total Carbohydrate: 71.4 g
- Protein: 28.3 g

17. Baked Shells in Sauce

"A filling main dish that is easily adaptable to suit your personal tastes. Recipe doubles/triples well. Use your favorite store bought or homemade tomato sauce."

Serving: 2 | Prep: 10 m | Cook: 30 m | Ready in: 40 m

Ingredients

- 1/2 cup seashell pasta
- 1 cup tomato sauce
- 1/2 cup mushrooms, diced
- 1/4 cup crumbled firm silken tofu
- 1/4 cup shredded mozzarella cheese
- 2 tablespoons grated Parmesan cheese

Direction

- Bring a pot of lightly salted water to a boil. Add pasta and cook for 8 to 10 minutes or until al dente; drain.
- Preheat oven to 400 degrees F (200 degrees C).
- In a medium bowl combine tomato sauce, mushrooms and tofu. Stir in cooked pasta. In a separate, small bowl combine mozzarella and Parmesan cheeses.
- In a small casserole dish layer pasta mixture and cheeses.
- Bake in preheated oven for 30 minutes, or until lightly browned.

Nutrition Information

- Calories: 212 calories
- Total Fat: 5.5 g
- Cholesterol: 13 mg

- Sodium: 819 mg
- Total Carbohydrate: 29.5 g
- Protein: 13.3 g

18. Balsamic Vinegar Tofu and Asparagus Pasta Salad

"Very tasty and good cold."

Serving: 6 | Prep: 10 m | Cook: 45 m | Ready in: 55 m

Ingredients

- 1 (12 ounce) package extra-firm tofu, cut into 1x2x2-inch pieces
- 1 pound fresh asparagus, trimmed
- 1 (16 ounce) package bow-tie pasta (farfalle)
- 1/4 cup extra-virgin olive oil
- 1/4 cup balsamic vinegar
- 1 pound grape tomatoes, halved
- 1 cup crumbled feta cheese
- 2 tablespoons chopped fresh basil, or more to taste

Direction

- Preheat oven to 400 degrees F (200 degrees C). Arrange tofu on a baking sheet.
- Cook tofu in the preheated oven until cooked through and lightly browned, about 20 minutes.
- Bring a large pot of lightly salted water to a boil. Add asparagus and cook uncovered until tender yet firm to the bite, 3 to 5 minutes. Drain.
- Bring a large pot of lightly salted water to a boil. Cook the bow-tie pasta at a boil, stirring occasionally, until cooked through yet

firm to the bite, about 12 minutes; drain and transfer pasta to a serving bowl.
- Heat olive oil and balsamic vinegar in a skillet over medium-high heat; fry tofu until liquid has reduced and tofu is slightly crisp, 2 to 3 minutes.
- Mix tofu, asparagus, tomatoes, feta cheese, and basil together with pasta.

Nutrition Information

- Calories: 498 calories
- Total Fat: 19.4 g
- Cholesterol: 22 mg
- Sodium: 298 mg
- Total Carbohydrate: 64.4 g
- Protein: 20.4 g

19. Black Bean Lasagna II

"Lasagna with a Southwest twist. This can be frozen unbaked and kept for up to a month. Simply thaw in refrigerator overnight and bake as directed. Tastes even better reheated the second day!"

Serving: 8 | Prep: 45 m | Cook: 45 m | Ready in: 1 h 30 m

Ingredients

- 9 lasagna noodles
- 1/2 cup chopped onion
- 1/2 cup chopped red bell pepper
- 1/2 cup frozen corn kernels, thawed
- 2 cloves garlic, chopped
- 1 (15 ounce) can black beans, rinsed and drained
- 1 (16 ounce) can refried black beans
- 2 3/4 cups canned tomato sauce
- 1/2 cup salsa
- 1/2 cup chopped fresh cilantro, divided
- 1 1/2 cups cottage cheese
- 1 cup ricotta cheese
- 1/4 cup sour cream
- 8 ounces Monterey Jack cheese, shredded
- 1/4 cup sliced ripe olives
- 8 sprigs fresh cilantro

Direction

- Preheat oven to 350 degrees F (175 degrees C). Bring a large pot of lightly salted water to a boil. Add pasta and cook for 8 to 10 minutes or until al dente; drain.

- Coat a large skillet with non-stick cooking spray, and place over medium heat. Sauté onion, red bell pepper, corn and garlic until tender. Stir in black beans, refried beans, tomato sauce, salsa and 1/4 cup cilantro. Cook until heated through and slightly thickened; set aside.
- In a large bowl, combine cottage cheese, ricotta, sour cream, shredded Monterey Jack cheese and remaining 1/4 cup chopped cilantro; set aside.
- Coat a 9x13 inch casserole dish with non-stick cooking spray. Arrange 3 of the cooked lasagna noodles in the bottom of the dish, cutting to fit if necessary. Spread with 1/3 of the bean mixture, then 1/3 of the cheese mixture. Repeat layers twice more.
- Cover, and bake in preheated oven for 45 minutes. Garnish with sliced black olives and sprigs of cilantro.

Nutrition Information

- Calories: 361 calories
- Total Fat: 14.4 g
- Cholesterol: 35 mg
- Sodium: 1067 mg
- Total Carbohydrate: 39.7 g
- Protein: 20.9 g

20. Bleu Cheese Macaroni

"This is not your average mac and cheese! Macaroni is combined with a creamy mixture of bleu cheese, Parmesan cheese and yogurt, and served with green and red bell peppers."

Serving: 6 | Prep: 5 m | Cook: 20 m | Ready in: 25 m

Ingredients

- 2 cups uncooked elbow macaroni
- 2 tablespoons butter
- 1 teaspoon salt
- 1/2 teaspoon black pepper
- 1/2 cup sliced green bell pepper
- 1/2 cup sliced red bell pepper
- 3/4 cup heavy cream
- 1/3 cup all-purpose flour
- 1/2 cup plain yogurt
- 1 cup crumbled blue cheese
- 1/2 cup grated Parmesan cheese

Direction

- Bring a large pot of lightly salted water to a boil. Add macaroni and cook for 8 to 10 minutes or until al dente; drain.
- Meanwhile, in a medium saucepan over medium heat combine butter, salt, pepper and bell peppers. Simmer until heated through. Stir in cream, flour, yogurt, bleu cheese and Parmesan cheese.
- Stir cooked macaroni into cheese mixture and serve hot.

Nutrition Information

- Calories: 433 calories
- Total Fat: 24.9 g
- Cholesterol: 76 mg
- Sodium: 883 mg
- Total Carbohydrate: 36.5 g
- Protein: 15.7 g

21. Bow Tie Medley

"This is a great recipe for a vegetarian pasta dish full of flavor."

Serving: 12 | Prep: 25 m | Cook: 20 m | Ready in: 45 m

Ingredients

- 1 (16 ounce) package farfalle (bow tie) pasta
- 1 tablespoon olive oil
- 1/2 red onion, chopped
- 4 cloves garlic, minced
- 1 zucchini, chopped
- 1 yellow squash, chopped
- 1/2 cup sliced fresh mushrooms
- 1/2 red bell pepper, cut into strips
- 5 roma (plum) tomatoes, chopped
- 1/4 cup fresh basil leaves
- 1 teaspoon dried oregano
- 1 teaspoon salt
- 1 teaspoon pepper
- 1/4 cup olive oil
- 1 cup finely grated Parmesan cheese

Direction

- Bring a large pot of lightly salted water to a boil. Add pasta and cook for 8 to 10 minutes or until al dente; drain.
- Heat 1 tablespoon olive oil in a large skillet over medium heat. Sauté onion, garlic, zucchini, yellow squash, mushrooms, bell pepper, and 1/2 the chopped tomatoes until tender. Season with basil, oregano, salt and pepper. Add pasta and 1/4 cup

olive oil. Mix well, and heat through. Sprinkle top with Parmesan and remaining chopped tomatoes.

Nutrition Information

- Calories: 243 calories
- Total Fat: 8.6 g
- Cholesterol: 6 mg
- Sodium: 301 mg
- Total Carbohydrate: 32.7 g
- Protein: 8.9 g

22. Broccoli Lasagna

"Broccoli lasagna with ricotta and mozzarella in a white sauce."

Serving: 6 | Prep: 20 m | Cook: 40 m | Ready in: 1 h

Ingredients

- 9 lasagna noodles
- 3 tablespoons butter
- 1 small onion, chopped
- 2 cloves garlic, chopped
- 2 tablespoons all-purpose flour
- 1/4 teaspoon ground white pepper
- 1 teaspoon salt, divided
- 1/8 teaspoon ground nutmeg
- 2 1/2 cups milk
- 2 tablespoons chopped fresh parsley
- 1 (15 ounce) container ricotta cheese
- 1 (10 ounce) package chopped frozen broccoli, thawed and drained
- 1/4 cup grated Parmesan cheese
- 2 cups shredded mozzarella cheese, divided

Direction

- Preheat oven to 350 degrees F (175 degrees C).
- Bring a large pot of lightly salted water to a boil. Add pasta and cook for 8 to 10 minutes or until al dente; drain.
- In a medium saucepan over medium heat, melt butter. Cook onion and garlic in butter until tender. Stir in flour, pepper, 1/2 teaspoon salt and nutmeg. Stirring continuously, pour in milk, a

little at a time, allowing mixture to thicken. Bring to a boil for 1 minute, then remove from heat and stir in parsley. Set aside.
- In a medium bowl, combine ricotta, broccoli, Parmesan, 1 cup of mozzarella and remaining 1/2 teaspoon salt. Stir until well blended.
- In a 7x11 inch baking dish layer: 1/4 cup white sauce; 3 noodles; one-third of remaining white sauce; half the broccoli mixture; 3 more noodles; half remaining white sauce; remaining broccoli mixture; 3 noodles; remaining white sauce. Sprinkle with remaining mozzarella. Cover with foil coated with cooking spray.
- Bake in preheated oven 30 minutes. Let stand 10 minutes before serving.

Nutrition Information

- Calories: 468 calories
- Total Fat: 21.4 g
- Cholesterol: 72 mg
- Sodium: 858 mg
- Total Carbohydrate: 41.7 g
- Protein: 28.6 g

23. Broccoli with Rigatoni

"A light and quick meal! To complete the meal serve with a side salad and garlic bread. Perfect!"

Serving: 5

Ingredients

- 8 tablespoons olive oil
- 2 tablespoons butter
- 4 cloves garlic, minced
- 1 pound fresh broccoli florets
- 1 cup vegetable broth
- 1 cup chopped fresh basil
- 1 pound rigatoni pasta
- 2 tablespoons grated Parmesan cheese

Direction

- Cook pasta according to package directions. Drain.
- In large skillet heat oil and butter. Gently brown garlic, add broccoli and sauté gently for 2 to 3 minutes. Add broth; cover and simmer until broccoli is tender.
- Toss the broccoli mixture with the basil and cooked pasta. Serve with grated Parmesan cheese on top.

Nutrition Information

- Calories: 608 calories
- Total Fat: 29.4 g
- Cholesterol: 14 mg

- Sodium: 191 mg
- Total Carbohydrate: 74.2 g
- Protein: 16.1 g

24. Broth Pesto with Pasta Peas and Chicken

"A deliciously creamy pasta dish that doesn't use any cream. The vegetable broth mixed with fresh pesto makes a very flavorful sauce. You can use real chicken but you should try the Quorn® stuff -- it's really good."

Serving: 4 | Prep: 10 m | Cook: 25 m | Ready in: 35 m

Ingredients

- 4 cups reduced-sodium vegetable broth
- 1 (8 ounce) package seashell pasta
- 1 tablespoon butter
- 2 tablespoons chopped spring onions
- 1 (12 ounce) package Quorn™ Chicken-Style Recipe Tenders
- 1 cup sweet peas
- 3 tablespoons pesto sauce, or more to taste

Direction

- Place the vegetable broth into a saucepan, and bring to a boil. Stir in the pasta, and boil over medium-low heat until tender, about 8 minutes. Drain pasta, and reserve broth.
- Heat the butter in a skillet over medium heat, and stir in half the spring onions; cook and stir until the onions begin to soften, 2 to 3 minutes, then add the vegetarian chicken-style pieces. Cook until vegetarian pieces are browned, about 3 minutes per side, then stir in remaining onion and green peas. Pour 1/2 cup of reserved vegetable broth into the skillet. Bring the mixture to a boil, cook for 1 to 2 minutes to cook the peas, and stir in the

pasta and pesto sauce. Mix in an additional 1/2 cup of broth to form a creamy sauce.

Nutrition Information

- Calories: 417 calories
- Total Fat: 11.5 g
- Cholesterol: 11 mg
- Sodium: 741 mg
- Total Carbohydrate: 59.1 g
- Protein: 23.2 g

25. Cajun Pasta Fresca

"This is my absolute favorite dish! If you like food with just a little kick and you are a pasta fan...this recipe is for you!"

Serving: 8 | Prep: 5 m | Cook: 20 m | Ready in: 25 m

Ingredients

- 1 pound vermicelli pasta
- 2 tablespoons olive oil
- 1 teaspoon minced garlic
- 13 roma (plum) tomatoes, chopped
- 1 tablespoon salt
- 1 tablespoon chopped fresh parsley
- 1 tablespoon Cajun seasoning
- 1/2 cup shredded mozzarella cheese
- 1/2 cup grated Parmesan cheese

Direction

- Bring a large pot of lightly salted water to a boil. Add pasta and cook for 8 to 10 minutes or until al dente; drain.
- While the pasta water is boiling, in a large skillet over medium heat, briefly sauté garlic in oil. Stir in tomatoes and their juice and sprinkle with salt. When tomatoes are bubbly, mash slightly with a fork. Stir in parsley, reduce heat and simmer 5 minutes more.
- Toss hot pasta with tomato sauce, Cajun seasoning, mozzarella and Parmesan.

Nutrition Information

- Calories: 294 calories
- Total Fat: 7.5 g
- Cholesterol: 9 mg
- Sodium: 1178 mg
- Total Carbohydrate: 46.2 g
- Protein: 12.2 g

26. Carries Artichoke and SunDried Tomato Pasta

"A versatile pasta dish with a wine based sauce: prawns and chicken are excellent additions to this recipe."

Serving: 4 | Prep: 30 m | Cook: 15 m | Ready in: 45 m

Ingredients

- 1 (8 ounce) package fresh fettuccine
- 4 tablespoons butter
- 1/2 medium onion, chopped
- 1 (8 ounce) package sliced mushrooms
- 3 cloves garlic, crushed
- 2/3 (8 ounce) jar sun-dried tomatoes, packed in oil
- 1 (2 ounce) can sliced black olives, drained
- 10 ounces marinated artichoke hearts
- 1 cup dry white wine
- 2 tablespoons lemon juice
- 1 ripe tomato, chopped
- 1 cup Parmesan cheese
- 1 teaspoon black pepper

Direction

- Fill a large pot with lightly salted water and bring it to a rolling boil.
- While the water is heating, melt the butter over medium heat in a large saucepan. Add the onions, mushrooms, and garlic; cook and stir until tender, about 5 minutes.

- Stir in the sun-dried tomatoes, olives, artichoke hearts, wine, and lemon juice. Bring to a boil; reduce the heat and simmer until liquid is reduced by a third, about 4 minutes.
- Cook the fresh pasta in boiling water until done, about 2 minutes. Drain.
- Toss pasta with sauce. Top with fresh tomatoes and cheese, add pepper to taste, and serve.

Nutrition Information

- Calories: 611 calories
- Total Fat: 29.5 g
- Cholesterol: 94 mg
- Sodium: 888 mg
- Total Carbohydrate: 61.1 g
- Protein: 21.3 g

27. Cathis Florentine Zucchini

"A simple, delicious pasta that my friend Cathi created while living in Florence. Flavors you wouldn't think to combine mix wonderfully. Don't use large, woody zucchini, but nice, young tender ones. The fresher the ricotta, the better. How much you reduce the wine depends on your ricotta: if you have fresh, slightly runny ricotta you need to let the wine reduce a little more than half, maybe two thirds, or your end product will be runny. And use a pasta with nooks to hold the sauce."

Serving: 8 | Prep: 10 m | Cook: 30 m | Ready in: 40 m

Ingredients

- 1 pound seashell pasta
- 2 tablespoons olive oil
- 1 onion, chopped
- 3 cloves garlic, chopped
- 4 zucchini, cut into 1/2-inch slices
- salt and pepper to taste
- 2/3 cup white wine
- 1/2 pound ricotta cheese
- 1/4 teaspoon ground cinnamon

Direction

- Bring a large pot of lightly salted water to a boil. Add pasta and cook for 8 to 10 minutes or until al dente; drain.
- Meanwhile, heat oil in a medium skillet over medium heat. Sauté onion and garlic until onions begin to soften. Stir in zucchini and season with salt and pepper.
- Increase the heat to medium-high and add the wine. Allow it to reduce by half, stirring frequently. Reduce heat to medium-low

and stir in ricotta and cinnamon. Heat through and season with salt and pepper. Add drained pasta to skillet and toss. Serve immediately.

Nutrition Information

- Calories: 311 calories
- Total Fat: 7.1 g
- Cholesterol: 9 mg
- Sodium: 43 mg
- Total Carbohydrate: 48 g
- Protein: 12.2 g

28. Cheese Lasagna

"An easy vegetarian lasagna with ricotta, mozzarella and Parmesan."

Serving: 8 | Prep: 20 m | Cook: 45 m | Ready in: 1 h 5 m

Ingredients

- 1 (16 ounce) package lasagna noodles
- 4 cups ricotta cheese
- 1/4 cup grated Parmesan cheese
- 4 eggs
- salt and pepper to taste
- 1 teaspoon olive oil
- 3 cloves garlic, minced
- 1 (32 ounce) jar spaghetti sauce
- 1 teaspoon Italian seasoning
- 2 cups shredded mozzarella cheese

Direction

- Preheat oven to 350 degrees F (175 degrees C). Bring a large pot of lightly salted water to a boil. Add pasta and cook for 8 to 10 minutes or until al dente; drain and lay lasagna flat on foil to cool.
- In a medium bowl, combine ricotta, Parmesan, eggs, salt and pepper; mix well.
- In a medium saucepan, heat oil over medium heat and sauté garlic for 2 minutes; stir in spaghetti sauce and Italian seasoning. Heat sauce until warmed through, stirring occasionally, 2 to 5 minutes.

- Spread 1/2 cup of sauce in the bottom of a 9x13 baking dish. Cover with a layer of noodles. Spread half the ricotta mixture over noodles; top with another noodle layer. Pour 1 1/2 cups of sauce over noodles, and spread the remaining ricotta over the sauce. Top with remaining noodles and sauce and sprinkle mozzarella over all. Cover with greased foil.
- Bake 45 minutes, or until cheese is bubbly and top is golden.

Nutrition Information

- Calories: 436 calories
- Total Fat: 14.4 g
- Cholesterol: 120 mg
- Sodium: 711 mg
- Total Carbohydrate: 57.6 g
- Protein: 19.8 g

29. Cheesy One Pan Mac And Cheese from Barilla

"Enjoy this delightfully cheesy version of classic Mac Cheese. Quick and easy!"

Serving: 6 | Prep: 5 m | Cook: 10 m | Ready in: 15 m

Ingredients

- 1 box Barilla® Pronto™ Rotini
- 1/2 tablespoon dry mustard
- 1 cup heavy cream
- 1 1/2 cups sharp Cheddar cheese, shredded
- 3/4 cup Parmigiano-Reggiano cheese, grated
- 2 tablespoons parsley, chopped
- Salt and black pepper to taste

Direction

- POUR whole box of pasta into a large skillet (approximately 12 inches in diameter).
- POUR 3 cups of cold water into the pan, ensuring that the water covers the pasta.
- Turn the burner to high, then set your timer for 10 minutes (optional: add a bit of salt to taste).
- COOK on high, stirring occasionally, until almost all of the liquid has evaporated.
- ADD dry mustard and cream and bring to a simmer then, REMOVE the skillet from heat and gently FOLD in the sharp cheddar, Parmigiano and parsley.
- Serve immediately.

Nutrition Information

- Calories: 526 calories
- Total Fat: 30.3 g
- Cholesterol: 99 mg
- Sodium: 409 mg
- Total Carbohydrate: 44.7 g
- Protein: 20.6 g

30. Cheesy Spinach Casserole

"A wonderful dish for parties or for home. This dish has a strong spinach and Monterey Jack cheese flavor, with a hint of artichoke and onion."

Serving: 4 | Prep: 10 m | Cook: 40 m | Ready in: 50 m

Ingredients

- 6 ounces uncooked spaghetti
- 1 egg
- 1/4 cup milk
- 1/2 cup sour cream
- 1 (10 ounce) package frozen chopped spinach, thawed
- 1/2 (14 ounce) can artichoke hearts, drained and chopped
- 1 (8 ounce) package shredded Monterey Jack cheese
- 4 tablespoons grated Parmesan cheese, divided
- 1 teaspoon dried minced onion
- salt and pepper to taste
- paprika to taste

Direction

- Bring a large pot of lightly salted water to a boil. Cook spaghetti in boiling water for 8 to 10 minutes, or until al dente; drain. Preheat oven to 350 degrees F (175 degrees C).
- In a 2 quart casserole dish, whisk together egg, milk, and sour cream. Using a wooden spoon, stir in spinach, artichoke hearts, Monterey Jack cheese, 2 tablespoons Parmesan cheese, and cooked spaghetti. Season with minced onion, salt, and pepper. Top with a sprinkling of paprika and remaining Parmesan cheese.

- Cover, and bake in preheated oven for 15 minutes. Remove cover, and bake for another 15 minutes. Let stand 2 minutes before serving.

Nutrition Information

- Calories: 522 calories
- Total Fat: 27 g
- Cholesterol: 115 mg
- Sodium: 1059 mg
- Total Carbohydrate: 42.6 g
- Protein: 28.5 g

31. Cheesy Vegetable Lasagna

"A rich, cheesy lasagna loaded with vegetables. You could also omit all veggies except broccoli for a broccoli lasagna."

Serving: 12 | Prep: 35 m | Cook: 35 m | Ready in: 1 h 20 m

Ingredients

- 12 lasagna noodles
- 2 tablespoons olive oil
- 2 heads fresh broccoli, chopped
- 2 carrots, thinly sliced
- 1 large onion, chopped
- 2 green bell peppers, chopped
- 2 small zucchini, sliced
- 3 cloves garlic, minced
- 1/2 cup all-purpose flour
- 3 cups milk
- 3/4 cup Parmesan cheese, divided
- 1/2 teaspoon salt
- 1/2 teaspoon pepper
- 1 (10 ounce) package frozen chopped spinach, thawed
- 1 (8 ounce) container small curd cottage cheese
- 24 ounces ricotta cheese
- 2 1/2 cups shredded mozzarella cheese, divided

Direction

- Preheat oven to 375 degrees F (190 degrees C). Grease a 9x13-inch casserole dish.

- Bring a large pot of lightly salted water to a boil. Add lasagna noodles and cook for 8 to 10 minutes or until al dente; drain.
- Heat oil in a large cast iron skillet over medium heat. When oil is hot add broccoli, carrots, onions, bell peppers, zucchini and garlic. Sauté for 7 minutes; set aside.
- Place flour in a medium saucepan and gradually whisk in milk until well blended. Bring to a boil over medium heat. Cook 5 minutes, or until thick, stirring constantly. Stir in 1/2 cup Parmesan cheese, salt and pepper; cook for 1 minute, stirring constantly. Remove from heat; stir in spinach. Reserve 1/2 cup spinach mixture. In a small bowl, combine cottage and ricotta cheeses; stir well.
- Spread about 1/2 cup of spinach mixture in the bottom of the prepared pan. Layer noodles, ricotta mixture, vegetables, spinach mixture, and 2 cups mozzarella cheese, ending with noodles. Top with reserved spinach mixture, 1/2 cup mozzarella cheese and 1/4 cup parmesan cheese.
- Bake in preheated oven for 35 minutes, or until lightly browned on top. Cool for approximately 10 minutes before serving.

Nutrition Information

- Calories: 375 calories
- Total Fat: 14.9 g
- Cholesterol: 45 mg
- Sodium: 530 mg
- Total Carbohydrate: 37 g
- Protein: 25 g

32. Cherry Tomato Sauce with Penne

"The best ways to eat cherry tomatoes are as follows: plucked warm off the vine and eaten raw standing in front of the plant. Next best is raw, in some sort of salad. Third best is made into a sauce as I've done here. Ladle into bowls and top with Parmigiano-Reggiano."

Serving: 4 | Prep: 15 m | Cook: 25 m | Ready in: 40 m

Ingredients

- 2 cups cherry tomatoes (such as Sun Gold)
- 2 tablespoons olive oil
- 2 cloves garlic, sliced
- salt and ground black pepper to taste
- 2 cups chicken broth
- 2 tablespoons fresh oregano leaves
- 1/2 teaspoon red pepper flakes
- 14 ounces penne pasta
- 1/2 cup grated Parmigiano-Reggiano cheese

Direction

- Combine cherry tomatoes, oil, garlic, and salt in a saucepan over medium-low heat. Cook and stir until garlic is just toasted, 2 to 3 minutes.
- Pour chicken broth into tomato mixture; bring to a simmer and cook until tomatoes start to collapse and burst, about 10 minutes. Stir oregano and red pepper flakes into tomato mixture.

- Puree tomato mixture with a stick blender until sauce is smooth.
- Bring a large pot of lightly salted water to a boil; add penne and cook, stirring occasionally, until tender yet firm to the bite, about 11 minutes. Drain and return pasta to the pot. Pour tomato sauce over penne and stir until pasta absorbs some of the sauce, 1 to 2 minutes. Stir Parmigiano-Reggiano cheese into pasta and season with salt and pepper to taste.

Nutrition Information

- Calories: 475 calories
- Total Fat: 12.3 g
- Cholesterol: 9 mg
- Sodium: 204 mg
- Total Carbohydrate: 76.2 g
- Protein: 17.7 g

33. Cheryls Spinach Cheesy Pasta Casserole

"This recipe was given by a friend and it instantly became a favorite! It tastes great as leftovers as well! Enjoy!"

Serving: 12 | Prep: 15 m | Cook: 1 h | Ready in: 1 h 15 m

Ingredients

- 1 (12 ounce) package medium seashell pasta
- 1 (10 ounce) package frozen chopped spinach, thawed
- 2 eggs
- 1/4 cup olive oil
- 1/2 cup bread crumbs
- 1 1/2 (26 ounce) jars tomato basil pasta sauce
- 1 (8 ounce) package shredded Cheddar cheese
- 1 (8 ounce) package shredded mozzarella cheese

Direction

- Preheat oven to 350 degrees F (175 degrees C).
- Bring a large pot of lightly salted water to a boil. Cook pasta in boiling water for 8 to 10 minutes, or until al dente; drain. Bring 1/2 cup water to a boil in a saucepan, and cook the spinach 4 to 6 minutes, until tender.
- Place the cooked pasta in a medium bowl. In a small bowl, whisk together the eggs and oil. Toss the pasta with the cooked spinach, egg mixture, and bread crumbs.
- Cover the bottom of a 9x13 inch baking dish with 1/3 of the pasta sauce. Pour half of the pasta mixture into the baking

dish, and cover with another 1/3 of the pasta sauce. Sprinkle with half of the Cheddar cheese and half of the mozzarella. Layer with remaining pasta mixture, and top with remaining sauce. Sprinkle with the rest of the Cheddar and mozzarella cheeses.
- Bake 45 minutes in the preheated oven, or until bubbly and lightly browned.

Nutrition Information

- Calories: 378 calories
- Total Fat: 18 g
- Cholesterol: 64 mg
- Sodium: 668 mg
- Total Carbohydrate: 38 g
- Protein: 17 g

34. Chickn Parmesan Casserole

"A vegetarian take on an American-Italian classic. Super easy and tasty."

Serving: 8 | Prep: 10 m | Cook: 35 m | Ready in: 45 m

Ingredients

- 2 (15 ounce) cans tomato sauce
- 1 teaspoon dried basil
- 1 teaspoon extra-virgin olive oil
- 1/4 cup grated Parmesan cheese
- 1 clove garlic, minced
- 1 dash white pepper
- 1/2 (16 ounce) package uncooked rotini pasta
- 1/2 (12 ounce) package artificial chicken tenders (such as Quorn™ Chik'n Tenders), cut in half
- 1/2 cup shredded mozzarella cheese

Direction

- Preheat an oven to 325 degrees F (165 degrees C).
- Bring the tomato sauce, basil, olive oil, Parmesan cheese, garlic, and white pepper to a simmer in a saucepan over medium-high heat. Reduce heat to low, and keep at a simmer. Fill a large pot with lightly salted water and bring to a rolling boil over high heat. Once the water is boiling, stir in the rotini, and return to a boil. Cook uncovered, stirring occasionally, until the pasta has cooked through, but is still firm to the bite, about 8 minutes. When the rotini is nearly ready, stir in the artificial chicken. Drain well.

- Spread half of the pasta sauce into the bottom of a 2 quart casserole dish, then add the drained pasta mixture. Pour the remaining sauce on top of the pasta, then sprinkle with the mozzarella cheese. Bake in the preheated oven until the cheese is bubbly and lightly browned, about 20 minutes.

Nutrition Information

- Calories: 188 calories
- Total Fat: 3.5 g
- Cholesterol: 7 mg
- Sodium: 722 mg
- Total Carbohydrate: 29.4 g
- Protein: 10.8 g

35. Chucks Favorite Mac and Cheese

"Easily doubled for a potluck, cottage cheese and sour cream are the unique elements to this macaroni and cheese recipe."

Serving: 6 | Prep: 10 m | Cook: 45 m | Ready in: 55 m

Ingredients

- 1 (8 ounce) package elbow macaroni
- 1 (8 ounce) package shredded sharp Cheddar cheese
- 1 (12 ounce) container small curd cottage cheese
- 1 (8 ounce) container sour cream
- 1/4 cup grated Parmesan cheese
- salt and pepper to taste
- 1 cup dry bread crumbs
- 1/4 cup butter, melted

Direction

- Preheat oven to 350 degrees F (175 degrees C). Bring a large pot of lightly salted water to a boil, add pasta, and cook until done; drain.
- In 9x13 inch baking dish, stir together macaroni, shredded Cheddar cheese, cottage cheese, sour cream, Parmesan cheese, salt and pepper. In a small bowl, mix together bread crumbs and melted butter. Sprinkle topping over macaroni mixture.
- Bake 30 to 35 minutes, or until top is golden.

Nutrition Information

- Calories: 591 calories
- Total Fat: 33.3 g
- Cholesterol: 88 mg
- Sodium: 720 mg
- Total Carbohydrate: 45.5 g
- Protein: 26.8 g

36. Convenient Vegetarian Lasagna

"This is a very easy to fix meal with lots of vegetables and no meat. Serve with a tossed green salad and some warm bread, if desired."

Serving: 12 | Prep: 30 m | Cook: 1 h | Ready in: 1 h 45 m

Ingredients

- 2 (12 ounce) packages lasagna noodles
- 2 pounds ricotta cheese
- 4 eggs
- 1 cup grated Parmesan cheese
- 1/3 cup chopped fresh parsley
- 2 teaspoons dried basil
- ground black pepper to taste
- 1/2 cup olive oil
- 1 1/2 cups chopped onion
- 1 cup sliced carrots
- 1 1/4 cups chopped green bell pepper
- 1 (16 ounce) package chopped frozen broccoli, thawed and drained
- 3 cups chunky-style spaghetti sauce
- 2 cups shredded mozzarella cheese, divided

Direction

- Bring a large pot of lightly salted water to a boil. Add pasta and cook for 8 to 10 minutes or until al dente; drain and set aside.

- In a large bowl, combine ricotta cheese, eggs, Parmesan cheese, parsley, basil and ground black pepper. Stir to blend; set aside.
- Heat oil in a large saucepan over high heat. Sauté onions for about 5 minutes, stirring occasionally; add carrot slices and sauté about 2 minutes, then stir in green bell pepper and broccoli. Stir all together, reduce heat to medium and cook until tender, about 5 minutes. Scrape veggies into ricotta mix and mix well.
- Preheat oven to 350 degrees F (175 degrees C).
- Ladle 1 cup of spaghetti sauce into a 9x13 inch baking dish and spread evenly over the bottom. Place 2 strips of lasagna lengthwise in the dish, then spread about 4 cups of the filling over the pasta. Sprinkle 1 cup of the mozzarella cheese over the filling; repeat layers.
- Bake at 350 degrees F (175 degrees C) for 1 hour; let stand about 15 to 20 minutes, to firm up, before serving.

Nutrition Information

- Calories: 581 calories
- Total Fat: 28.9 g
- Cholesterol: 121 mg
- Sodium: 605 mg
- Total Carbohydrate: 55.3 g
- Protein: 27.4 g

37. Corny Spaghetti

"Family favorite for years, great way to get veggies into kids, and no separate side dishes. Top with fresh chopped parsley and/or parmesan if desired. This stuff reheats great and I have used ground beef in it before, just brown it with the onions, drain then continue recipe. I hope you all enjoy it as much as we have."

Serving: 6 | Prep: 5 m | Cook: 15 m | Ready in: 20 m

Ingredients

- 10 ounces angel hair pasta
- 2 tablespoons butter
- 1/2 red onion, chopped
- 1 teaspoon minced garlic
- 3 zucchini, diced
- 1 pound button mushrooms, quartered
- 1/4 cup red wine
- 1 (16 ounce) jar pasta sauce
- 1 (15 ounce) can whole kernel corn, drained

Direction

- Bring a large pot of lightly salted water to a boil. Add pasta and cook for 8 to 10 minutes or until al dente; drain.
- While pasta is cooking, in large skillet over medium heat, sauté onion in butter 2 minutes. Stir in garlic and zucchini and cook 3 minutes more. Add mushrooms and cook 5 minutes more, until mushrooms are soft. Pour in red wine and pasta sauce, reduce heat to low and simmer. Add corn and bring back to a simmer again to heat through.
- Serve sauce over pasta with a dab of butter, or toss together.

Nutrition Information

- Calories: 331 calories
- Total Fat: 8.2 g
- Cholesterol: 12 mg
- Sodium: 643 mg
- Total Carbohydrate: 56.2 g
- Protein: 10.9 g

38. Couscous Gourmet

"This meal will satisfy anyone and appeal to the biggest food critic with a few simple tricks!"

Serving: 4 | Prep: 25 m | Cook: 15 m | Ready in: 45 m

Ingredients

- 1 1/4 cups water
- 1 (10 ounce) box whole wheat couscous with flaxseed
- 5 teaspoons butter
- 1 teaspoon chopped fresh basil, or to taste
- 1 tablespoon olive oil
- 1 pound fresh asparagus, trimmed and cut into thirds
- 1 zucchini, sliced
- 1 red bell pepper, cut into strips
- 1 clove garlic, minced
- salt and ground black pepper to taste
- 1 sprig fresh basil

Direction

- Bring water to a boil in a saucepan and stir in couscous. Bring back to a boil, reduce heat to low, cover the pan, and simmer couscous until water is absorbed, about 5 minutes. Remove from heat and allow to stand covered for about 5 more minutes to let couscous dry.
- Stir butter and 1 teaspoon basil lightly into couscous until butter is melted; set couscous aside.
- Heat olive oil in a skillet over medium heat; cook and stir asparagus, zucchini, red bell pepper, and garlic in the hot oil

until the vegetables are tender and just starting to brown, about 10 minutes. Season with salt and black pepper.
- Pack the couscous tightly into a measuring cup or bowl; place serving platter face down on top of the cup, invert the platter, and remove cup to turn couscous out onto the platter in a rounded shape.
- Arrange cooked vegetables around the mound of couscous; place 1 sprig of basil in center of couscous to serve.

Nutrition Information

- Calories: 399 calories
- Total Fat: 11.2 g
- Cholesterol: 13 mg
- Sodium: 45 mg
- Total Carbohydrate: 67.3 g
- Protein: 15.8 g

39. Couscous with Mushrooms and SunDried Tomatoes

"Lively sun-dried tomatoes and hearty portobello mushrooms are tossed with couscous in this satisfying entree."

Serving: 4 | Prep: 30 m | Cook: 15 m | Ready in: 45 m

Ingredients

- 1 cup dehydrated sun-dried tomatoes
- 1 1/2 cups water
- 1/2 (10 ounce) package couscous
- 1 teaspoon olive oil
- 3 cloves garlic, pressed
- 1 bunch green onions, chopped
- 1/3 cup fresh basil leaves
- 1/4 cup fresh cilantro, chopped
- 1/2 lemon, juiced
- salt and pepper to taste
- 4 ounces portobello mushroom caps, sliced

Direction

- Place the sun-dried tomatoes in a bowl with 1 cup water. Soak 30 minutes, until rehydrated. Drain, reserving water, and chop.
- In a medium saucepan, combine the reserved sun-dried tomato water with enough water to yield 1 1/2 cups. Bring to a boil. Stir in the couscous. Cover, remove from heat, and allow to sit 5 minutes, until liquid has been absorbed. Gently fluff with a fork.

- Heat the olive oil in a skillet. Stir in the sun-dried tomatoes, garlic, and green onions. Cook and stir about 5 minutes, until the green onions are tender. Mix in the basil, cilantro, and lemon juice. Season with salt and pepper. Mix in the mushrooms, and continue cooking 3 to 5 minutes. Toss with the cooked couscous to serve.

Nutrition Information

- Calories: 178 calories
- Total Fat: 2 g
- Cholesterol: 0 mg
- Sodium: 300 mg
- Total Carbohydrate: 36.1 g
- Protein: 7.5 g

40. Couscous with Olives and SunDried Tomato

"A delicate, flavorful dish that will satisfy vegans and carnivores alike! Inspired by my family's deep Coptic Orthodox Christian tradition, this is a great meal alternative during strict fasting times. It contains no animal products or fats, but has enough flavor and visual impact to make you feel like you're not sacrificing a thing! I hope you will enjoy this recipe. Add chicken or prawns to make this vegan dish a carnivorous delight!"

Serving: 4 | Prep: 20 m | Cook: 30 m | Ready in: 50 m

Ingredients

- 1 1/4 cups vegetable broth
- 1 1/4 cups water
- 2 cups pearl (Israeli) couscous
- 1 pinch salt
- 1 pinch ground black pepper
- 5 tablespoons olive oil, divided
- 1/2 cup pine nuts
- 4 cloves garlic, minced
- 1 shallot, minced
- 1/2 cup sliced black olives
- 1/3 cup sun-dried tomatoes packed in oil, drained and chopped
- 1 cup vegetable broth
- 1/4 cup chopped fresh flat-leaf parsley

Direction

- Bring 1 1/4 cup vegetable broth and water to a boil in a saucepan, stir in couscous, and mix in salt and black pepper.

Reduce heat to low and simmer until liquid is absorbed, about 8 minutes.
- Heat 3 tablespoons olive oil in a skillet over medium-high heat; stir in pine nuts and cook, stirring frequently, until pine nuts smell toasted and are golden brown, about 1 minute. Remove from heat.
- Heat remaining 2 tablespoons olive oil in a saucepan; cook and stir garlic and shallot in the hot oil until softened, about 2 minutes. Stir black olives and sun-dried tomatoes into garlic mixture and cook until heated through, 2 to 3 minutes, stirring often. Slowly pour in 1 cup vegetable broth and bring mixture to a boil. Reduce heat to low and simmer until sauce has reduced, 8 to 10 minutes.
- Transfer couscous to a large serving bowl, mix with sauce, and serve topped with parsley and pine nuts.

Nutrition Information

- Calories: 528 calories
- Total Fat: 29.3 g
- Cholesterol: 0 mg
- Sodium: 455 mg
- Total Carbohydrate: 55.5 g
- Protein: 13 g

41. Cranberry Butternut Squash Couscous

"A great fall or winter dish! Serve at room temperature."

Serving: 4 | Prep: 15 m | Cook: 25 m | Ready in: 55 m

Ingredients

- 2 cups fresh cranberries
- 2 tablespoons olive oil, divided
- 1 tablespoon white sugar
- 2 teaspoons chopped fresh thyme
- 4 cups peeled and diced butternut squash
- 1 teaspoon salt, divided
- 1/4 teaspoon ground black pepper
- 1 (10 ounce) box couscous
- 1/3 cup diced celery
- 4 tablespoons lemon juice
- 1 lemon, zested
- 2 teaspoons olive oil

Direction

- Preheat oven to 400 degrees F (200 degrees C).
- Toss cranberries with 2 teaspoons olive oil, sugar, and thyme in a bowl. Pour onto a baking sheet.
- Arrange butternut squash into a single layer on a separate baking sheet. Coat evenly with 1/4 teaspoon salt and pepper.
- Bake cranberries and squash in the preheated oven until cranberries are softened and lightly browned and squash is

tender, 15 to 20 minutes.
- Bring water to a boil in a saucepan; add 1 tablespoon olive oil and 1/2 teaspoon salt. Remove from heat and stir in couscous. Cover saucepan and let stand until water is absorbed completely, about 5 minutes. Fluff couscous with a fork; let cool for 10 minutes more.
- Combine the cranberries, butternut squash, couscous, celery, lemon juice, lemon zest, and the remaining 2 teaspoons olive oil and 1/4 teaspoon salt in a bowl.

Nutrition Information

- Calories: 451 calories
- Total Fat: 9.8 g
- Cholesterol: 0 mg
- Sodium: 603 mg
- Total Carbohydrate: 82.2 g
- Protein: 10.8 g

42. Creamy Artichoke Pasta

"This is a great fast and simple pasta dish, with a sauce that is lower in fat, yet creamy! If you like artichokes, you'll like this! You can adjust all the seasonings to suit your tastes."

Serving: 4 | Prep: 15 m | Cook: 15 m | Ready in: 30 m

Ingredients

- 12 ounces uncooked spaghetti
- 1 tablespoon olive oil
- 1 tablespoon butter
- 1 (6 ounce) can marinated artichoke hearts
- 1 small onion
- 3 cloves garlic, chopped
- 1/2 teaspoon salt
- 1/4 teaspoon ground black pepper
- 1/8 teaspoon ground cayenne pepper
- 1 teaspoon dried oregano
- 1/2 cup low-fat cottage cheese
- 1/2 cup low-fat sour cream
- 1/2 cup grated Parmesan cheese

Direction

- Bring a large pot of salted water to a boil. Add spaghetti and cook until al dente. Drain and keep warm.
- While pasta is cooking, heat a large skillet over medium-high heat. Place olive oil, butter, and liquid from artichoke hearts in skillet. Cut artichoke hearts into bite-size pieces. When olive oil mixture is hot, add onion and garlic. Sauté until soft and lightly

browned. Stir in artichoke hearts and sauté until heated through. Season with salt, black pepper, cayenne pepper, and oregano. Remove from heat and stir in cottage cheese and sour cream. Toss mixture with cooked pasta and top with Parmesan cheese.

Nutrition Information

- Calories: 536 calories
- Total Fat: 17.6 g
- Cholesterol: 33 mg
- Sodium: 793 mg
- Total Carbohydrate: 72.7 g
- Protein: 22.5 g

43. Creamy Asparagus Pasta

"A wonderfully satisfying meal that cooks in minutes. Delicious!"

Serving: 8 | Prep: 5 m | Cook: 25 m | Ready in: 30 m

Ingredients

- 1 pound fresh asparagus, trimmed and cut into 2 inch pieces
- 2 tablespoons butter
- 1 clove garlic, minced
- 1 pint light cream
- 1 pound linguine pasta
- 1 lemon, juiced

Direction

- Bring a pot of water to a boil. Boil asparagus for 3 to 4 minutes; drain.
- In a large saucepan melt butter over medium heat. Sauté garlic and asparagus for 3 to 4 minutes. Stir in the cream and simmer for 10 minutes.
- Meanwhile, bring a large pot of water to a boil. Add linguine and cook for 8 to 10 minutes or until al dente; drain and transfer to a serving dish.
- Stir lemon juice into asparagus mixture; pour mixture over pasta.

Nutrition Information

- Calories: 247 calories

- Total Fat: 4.7 g
- Cholesterol: 10 mg
- Sodium: 31 mg
- Total Carbohydrate: 44 g
- Protein: 8.3 g

44. Creamy Coconut Carbonara Without Milk

"Great for vegas! Tastes just like traditional Carbonara or even better! The coconut is very healthy! Enjoy this romantic, simple, hot dish!"

Serving: 2 | Prep: 20 m | Cook: 20 m | Ready in: 40 m

Ingredients

- 4 ounces fettuccine pasta
- 1 tablespoon vegetable oil
- 2 onions, coarsely chopped, or to taste
- 1 tablespoon minced garlic
- 1 cup coconut milk, divided
- 1/2 cup fresh oyster mushrooms, diced small
- 1/3 cup thinly sliced red bell pepper
- 1/3 cup thinly sliced green bell pepper
- salt and ground black pepper to taste
- 2 spring onions, sliced, or more to taste
- 1 tablespoon chopped fresh basil

Direction

- Fill a large pot with lightly salted water and bring to a rolling boil. Stir in fettuccine, bring back to a boil, and cook over medium heat until tender yet firm to the bite, about 8 minutes. Drain.
- Heat oil in a large saucepan over high heat. Add onion and garlic; cook, stirring constantly, until slightly browned, 2 to 4 minutes. Add 1/2 cup coconut milk, oyster mushrooms, red bell

- pepper, and green bell pepper. Cook and stir until just tender, 3 to 5 minutes.
- Stir fettuccine and remaining 1/2 cup coconut milk into the saucepan. Season with salt and pepper. Stir in spring onions and basil. Cook uncovered until sauce is creamy and coats fettuccine, 2 to 3 minutes more.

Nutrition Information

- Calories: 601 calories
- Total Fat: 32.6 g
- Cholesterol: 0 mg
- Sodium: 112 mg
- Total Carbohydrate: 70.4 g
- Protein: 13.7 g

45. Creamy Gorgonzola Spinach Pasta

"This is one of those super quick pasta recipes that is ready in about 20 minutes. Use any kind of pasta and serve with this creamy Gorgonzola sauce with fresh spinach."

Serving: 4 | Prep: 5 m | Cook: 15 m | Ready in: 20 m

Ingredients

- 1 (16 ounce) package fusilli pasta
- 1 1/2 tablespoons butter
- 2 shallots, minced
- 1 cup heavy whipping cream
- 4 cups fresh spinach
- 1/2 cup Gorgonzola cheese
- salt and freshly ground black pepper to taste

Direction

- Bring a large pot of lightly salted water to a boil. Cook fusilli in the boiling water, stirring occasionally, until tender yet firm to the bite, about 12 minutes.
- In the meantime, melt butter in a skillet over medium heat and cook shallots until soft and translucent, 3 to 5 minutes. Pour in cream and cook until heated through, 3 to 5 minutes. Add spinach and crumble in Gorgonzola cheese. Season with salt and pepper and cook until spinach is wilted and sauce has thickened, about 4 minutes.
- Drain fusilli and toss with sauce. Serve immediately.

Nutrition Information

- Calories: 730 calories
- Total Fat: 33.9 g
- Cholesterol: 111 mg
- Sodium: 293 mg
- Total Carbohydrate: 88.5 g
- Protein: 21.3 g

46. Creamy Pasta Bake with Cherry Tomatoes and Basil

"One of my favorite midweek pasta bakes - my whole family loves it and there is not much prep. Once the pasta bake is in the oven, you can make a salad or set the table and then it's time to eat."

Serving: 6 | Prep: 15 m | Cook: 31 m | Ready in: 46 m

Ingredients

- 1 (16 ounce) package penne pasta
- 1 tablespoon olive oil
- 1 onion, finely chopped
- 3 cloves garlic, minced
- 3 (6 ounce) cans tomato sauce
- 2 tablespoons tomato paste
- 3/4 cup heavy whipping cream
- 1/2 cup grated Parmesan cheese
- salt and freshly ground black pepper
- 1 pinch white sugar
- 1 pound cherry tomatoes, halved
- 1 1/4 cups shredded mozzarella cheese
- 1 small bunch fresh basil, finely chopped

Direction

- Bring a large pot of lightly salted water to a boil. Add penne and cook, stirring occasionally, until tender yet firm to the bite, about 11 minutes. Drain, reserving 1 cup of cooking water.
- Heat olive oil in a large skillet over medium heat and cook onion until soft and translucent while penne is cooking, about 5

minutes. Add garlic and cook an additional 30 seconds. Stir in tomato sauce and tomato paste and cook until slightly reduced, about 5 minutes. Add cream and Parmesan cheese and season with salt, pepper, and sugar.
- Preheat oven to 400 degrees F (200 degrees C). Grease a baking dish.
- Stir some pasta cooking water into the sauce and add cooked penne. Remove from heat and stir in cherry tomatoes, 1/2 the mozzarella cheese, and basil. Pour penne mixture into the prepared baking dish and cover with remaining mozzarella cheese.
- Bake in the preheated oven until cheese is melted, about 20 minutes.

Nutrition Information

- Calories: 532 calories
- Total Fat: 21.2 g
- Cholesterol: 62 mg
- Sodium: 780 mg
- Total Carbohydrate: 67.8 g
- Protein: 21.4 g

47. Creamy Spinach Tortellini

"Delicious tortellini is dressed up with tomatoes, mushrooms, spinach and a rich creamy sauce. A favorite pasta dish in our family!"

Serving: 4 | Prep: 15 m | Cook: 20 m | Ready in: 35 m

Ingredients

- 1 (9 ounce) package refrigerated cheese tortellini
- 2 tablespoons Butter
- 1 small onion, chopped
- 1 (8 ounce) package cream cheese
- 1/2 cup grated Parmesan cheese
- 1/2 cup milk
- fresh mushrooms, sliced
- 1 (10 ounce) package frozen chopped spinach, thawed and drained
- cherry tomatoes, halved

Direction

- Cook tortellini according to package directions.
- Heat butter in a large skillet over medium heat. Stir in onion; cook until soft and translucent. Mix in cream cheese, parmesan, milk, mushrooms, and spinach.
- Gently mix in tortellini and cherry tomatoes with skillet contents; warm through, and serve.

Nutrition Information

- Calories: 546 calories

- Total Fat: 35 g
- Cholesterol: 116 mg
- Sodium: 671 mg
- Total Carbohydrate: 40.2 g
- Protein: 21.8 g

48. Creamy SunDried Tomato Couscous

"This savory and satisfying one-pot meal is quick to make and devoured even faster! Great as a vegetarian entree or pairs well with any protein. Wonderful creamy texture without adding butter or cream. This will find its way into your weekly rotation!"

Serving: 4 | Prep: 20 m | Cook: 19 m | Ready in: 39 m

Ingredients

- 2 tablespoons extra-virgin olive oil
- 1/2 small sweet onion, chopped
- 1 small Chinese eggplant, chopped
- 1/2 zucchini, chopped
- 2 ounces baby bella mushrooms, chopped
- salt and ground black pepper to taste
- 2 ounces sun-dried tomatoes packed in oil, drained
- 2 cloves garlic, chopped
- 2 teaspoons dried basil
- 1 1/2 cups vegetable stock
- 1 cup tri-colored pearl couscous
- 2 tablespoons sun-dried tomato oil
- 1 tablespoon shaved Parmesan cheese, or to taste

Direction

- Heat olive oil in a large skillet over medium heat; cook and stir onion, eggplant, zucchini, mushrooms, salt, and pepper until onion is translucent, 5 to 7 minutes. Add tomatoes, garlic, and basil; cook and stir for 2 minutes.

- Pour vegetable stock into the skillet; bring to a boil. Add couscous, stir well, and cover skillet; simmer until couscous is tender yet firm to the bite, 7 to 10 minutes.
- Stir tomato oil into couscous mixture and top with Parmesan cheese.

Nutrition Information

- Calories: 357 calories
- Total Fat: 16.7 g
- Cholesterol: 1 mg
- Sodium: 207 mg
- Total Carbohydrate: 44.9 g
- Protein: 8.6 g

49. Creamy Zucchini with Linguine

"A different and delicious way to eat up all the zucchini that's overflowing from the garden. Diced zucchini are sauteed with garlic and red pepper flakes then simmered with cream, and served with Parmesan cheese and chopped parsley. Don't skimp on the olive oil."

Serving: 6 | Prep: 20 m | Cook: 30 m | Ready in: 50 m

Ingredients

- 1/2 cup olive oil
- 2 large zucchini, diced
- 2 cloves garlic, thinly sliced
- 1/2 teaspoon salt
- 1/8 teaspoon crushed red pepper flakes
- 1 (12 ounce) package linguine pasta
- 1 cup whole milk
- 2 tablespoons chopped fresh parsley
- 1/2 cup freshly grated Parmesan cheese

Direction

- Warm olive oil in a large skillet over medium heat. Add zucchini and garlic to hot oil, and season with salt and red pepper flakes. Cook, turning occasionally, until zucchini are well browned on all sides, about 20 minutes.
- Meanwhile, bring a large pot of generously salted water to boil. Add pasta, and cook until al dente, about 8 to 10 minutes. Drain, and set aside.

- Stir milk into zucchini, and simmer until it is reduced by about half, about 10 minutes. Add pasta to skillet, and stir well. Sprinkle parsley and 1/4 cup Parmesan over the top, and toss. Garnish with remaining Parmesan to serve.

Nutrition Information

- Calories: 429 calories
- Total Fat: 22.2 g
- Cholesterol: 10 mg
- Sodium: 318 mg
- Total Carbohydrate: 46.5 g
- Protein: 11.3 g

50. Crispy Chinese Noodles with Eggplant and Peanuts

"Chinese noodles are inexpensive to buy and can be found at your local supermarket. These noodles are fantastic! Eggplant, sherry and fresh ginger meld together to create a divine taste."

Serving: 4 | Prep: 30 m | Cook: 25 m | Ready in: 55 m

Ingredients

- 1 medium eggplant, cubed
- 1 teaspoon salt
- 16 ounces fresh Chinese wheat noodles
- 2 tablespoons sherry
- 1 tablespoon cornstarch
- 1/4 cup red wine vinegar
- 1/3 cup water
- 1 tablespoon minced fresh ginger root
- 1 tablespoon white sugar
- 2 tablespoons vegetarian fish sauce
- 2 cups sliced onion
- 3 tablespoons canola oil
- 4 cloves garlic, minced
- 1 red bell pepper, julienned
- 4 tablespoons chopped, unsalted dry-roasted peanuts
- 1 tablespoon chopped fresh mint (optional)

Direction

- Place the eggplant cubes into a colander. Add the salt and toss well. Let the eggplant drain for 15 minutes, then rinse it lightly

with water. Let the eggplant drain again in the colander.
- Bring a large pot of water to a boil. Add the noodles and boil them for about 5 minutes, until they are tender. Drain and rinse well with cold water. Let the noodles drain in a colander for at least 10 minutes.
- Combine the sherry with the cornstarch in a small bowl. Mix well and set aside.
- In a saucepan combine the red wine vinegar, water, ginger, sugar, imitation fish sauce, and onions. Bring the mixture to a boil, turn the heat to low and let the mixture simmer for 5 minutes.
- In a large skillet, preferably non-stick, heat 1 1/2 tablespoon oil over medium-high heat. Add the eggplant, and cook it for 5 minutes, stirring frequently. Add the garlic and red pepper and cook, stirring occasionally for 5 minutes more or until the eggplant softens. Add both the onion-vinegar mixture and the cornstarch-sherry mixture. Cook for 2 to 3 minutes, stirring occasionally. Keep the mixture warm.
- In a large non-stick skillet heat the remaining 1 1/2 tablespoons oil over medium-high heat. When the oil begins to smoke, add the noodles, then place two or three plates on top of them so that more surface area will brown. Let the noodles sit over medium-high heat for 5 minutes. When the noodles have developed a golden brown crust on the underside remove the plates, turn the noodles over with a spatula and cook them 5 minutes on the other side. Then take the pan off the heat.
- Add the peanuts to the eggplant mixture, and spoon it onto plates. Divide the noodles into four parts, and place them atop the vegetables and sauce. Sprinkle with mint, if you like, and serve.

Nutrition Information

- Calories: 558 calories
- Total Fat: 16.9 g
- Cholesterol: 0 mg
- Sodium: 1310 mg
- Total Carbohydrate: 88.2 g
- Protein: 12.3 g

51. Curried Couscous with Spinach and Chickpeas

"A quick, filling vegetarian meal. The vegetable broth makes it heartier than some couscous recipes. Serve with plain yogurt."

Serving: 4 | Prep: 20 m | Cook: 25 m | Ready in: 45 m

Ingredients

- 2 tablespoons olive oil
- 1 small yellow onion, chopped
- 1/2 cup chopped sun-dried tomatoes
- 1 tablespoon chopped fresh dill
- 3 cloves garlic, crushed
- 12 ounces chopped frozen spinach
- 1 tablespoon pale dry sherry
- 1 tablespoon curry powder
- 1 pinch cayenne pepper, or to taste
- 1 (15 ounce) can chickpeas, drained
- 2 cups vegetable broth
- 1 cup whole wheat couscous
- salt to taste

Direction

- Heat olive oil in a skillet over medium heat. Add onion, sun-dried tomato, dill, and garlic; cook and stir until onions start to turn translucent, about 5 minutes. Stir in spinach, increase heat to medium high, and cook until spinach begins to wilt, 5 to 10 minutes.

- Pour in sherry and cook until most liquid has evaporated, about 5 minutes. Add curry powder, cayenne pepper, chickpeas, and 1 cup of the vegetable broth; cook for about 5 minutes. Add remaining broth and bring mixture to a boil. Remove from heat, stir in couscous, and cover until couscous absorbs all the liquid, 5 to 10 minutes. Season with salt.

Nutrition Information

- Calories: 398 calories
- Total Fat: 6.2 g
- Cholesterol: 0 mg
- Sodium: 666 mg
- Total Carbohydrate: 74.6 g
- Protein: 16.5 g

52. Debbies Vegetable Lasagna

"Delicious vegetable lasagna with a white creamy sauce. A family favorite!"

Serving: 8 | Prep: 25 m | Cook: 45 m | Ready in: 1 h 10 m

Ingredients

- 9 lasagna noodles
- 1/4 cup margarine
- 1/4 cup all-purpose flour
- 1/2 teaspoon salt
- 1/4 teaspoon ground black pepper
- 1 cup milk
- 1/2 cup vegetable broth, or as needed
- 2 tablespoons white wine
- 1/2 cup grated Parmesan cheese
- 1 cup light ricotta cheese
- 1 egg
- 1 egg white
- 1 tablespoon olive oil
- 2 cups coarsely shredded carrots
- 2 cups coarsely chopped zucchini
- 1 (10 ounce) package frozen chopped spinach, thawed and drained
- 1 cup shredded mozzarella cheese

Direction

- Bring a large pot of lightly salted water to a boil. Cook lasagna in the boiling water, stirring occasionally until cooked through but firm to the bite, about 8 minutes. Drain.

- Preheat oven to 375 degrees F (190 degrees C).
- Melt margarine in a skillet over low heat; cook and stir flour, salt, and pepper into the melted margarine until smooth and bubbling, 2 to 3 minutes. Add milk and broth into flour mixture, stirring constantly; bring sauce to a boil. Stir wine into sauce and remove from heat. Stir Parmesan cheese into sauce until smooth.
- Whisk ricotta cheese, egg, and egg white together in a bowl.
- Heat olive oil in a skillet over medium-high heat; sauté carrots, zucchini, and spinach until just becoming tender, 5 to 10 minutes. Stir vegetable mixture into ricotta mixture.
- Layer 1/3 the lasagna noodles, 1/3 the ricotta-vegetable mixture, and 1/3 the Parmesan sauce in a 9x13-inch baking dish; repeat layering 2 more times with remaining ingredients, ending with a layer of mozzarella cheese.
- Bake in the preheated oven until cheese is lightly browned and bubbling, about 30 minutes.

Nutrition Information

- Calories: 291 calories
- Total Fat: 13.2 g
- Cholesterol: 39 mg
- Sodium: 482 mg
- Total Carbohydrate: 30.4 g
- Protein: 13.6 g

53. Delicious Angel Hair Pasta

"Angel hair pasta cooked and served with essentially a hot pasta salad dressing and cheese. I came up with this recipe as I could not find anything to eat, so I went through my spice cabinet and refrigerator, found these ingredients and threw them together. Serve with fresh chopped tomato."

Serving: 1 | Prep: 10 m | Cook: 10 m | Ready in: 20 m

Ingredients

- 1/4 (8 ounce) package angel hair pasta
- 1 tablespoon extra-virgin olive oil
- 2 tablespoons chopped pimentos
- 2 tablespoons lemon juice
- 1 teaspoon white wine vinegar
- 1 teaspoon white sugar
- 2 tablespoons chopped fresh parsley, divided
- 1 tablespoon chopped fresh basil
- 1 tablespoon chopped fresh oregano
- 1/4 teaspoon garlic powder
- 1/4 teaspoon onion powder
- 3 tablespoons grated Parmesan cheese
- salt and pepper to taste

Direction

- Bring a pot of lightly salted water to a rolling boil; cook the angel hair pasta in boiling water until the pasta has cooked through yet firm to the bite, 4 to 5 minutes. Drain.
- Heat the olive oil in a skillet over medium-high heat. Add the pimentos, lemon juice, vinegar, sugar, 1 tablespoon parsley,

basil, oregano, garlic powder, and onion powder to the oil and stir; cook until the herbs are heated and fragrant. Stir the Parmesan cheese into the mixture. Add the pasta to the skillet and toss to evenly coat with the seasonings. Season with salt and pepper, garnish with remaining parsley, and serve hot.

Nutrition Information

- Calories: 387 calories
- Total Fat: 19.6 g
- Cholesterol: 13 mg
- Sodium: 354 mg
- Total Carbohydrate: 41.7 g
- Protein: 12.8 g

54. Easy Fettucine Alfredo

"A quick, easy, and delicious low calorie Alfredo sauce that the family will love! Garnish with fresh basil and grated Parmesan cheese."

Serving: 4

Ingredients

- 8 ounces dry fettuccine pasta
- 1 tablespoon olive oil
- 1 cup evaporated skim milk
- 1/3 cup grated Parmesan cheese
- 1/2 teaspoon dried basil
- 1 1/2 lemons, juiced
- 1 pinch ground black pepper

Direction

- Cook pasta according to package directions. Drain; immediately return to pan. Add olive oil; toss to coat. Add evaporated milk, 1/3 cup Parmesan cheese, dried basil, lemon juice, and pepper. Cook over medium-high heat until bubbly, stirring constantly. Top with additional Parmesan cheese and fresh basil.

Nutrition Information

- Calories: 318 calories
- Total Fat: 6.8 g
- Cholesterol: 8 mg
- Sodium: 180 mg

- Total Carbohydrate: 52.9 g
- Protein: 15.4 g

55. Easy Pasta Bake with Leek and Cheese

"A quick and easy pasta bake with leek and cheese that I often make during the week. If you like, you can add ham or bacon to the noodles."

Serving: 4 | Prep: 10 m | Cook: 21 m | Ready in: 31 m

Ingredients

- 1 bunch leeks, quartered lengthwise and cut into 2-inch pieces
- 1/2 (16 ounce) box penne pasta
- 1 cup heavy cream
- 2 tablespoons butter
- 1 1/2 cups shredded Emmentaler cheese
- 1 pinch salt and freshly ground black pepper to taste

Direction

- Bring a large pot of lightly salted water to a boil. Add penne and cook, stirring occasionally, until tender yet firm to the bite, about 11 minutes. Drain.
- Bring a second large pot of lightly salted water to a boil and cook leek for 2 minutes while penne is cooking. Drain well.
- Preheat oven to 475 degrees F (245 degrees C). Grease a baking dish with some butter.
- Heat cream and butter in a saucepan over low heat until hot. Whisk in Emmentaler cheese until melted. Season with salt and pepper. Mix cooked penne and leek and add to the prepared baking dish. Pour cheese sauce on top.

- Bake in the preheated oven until lightly browned, about 10 minutes.

Nutrition Information

- Calories: 721 calories
- Total Fat: 43.2 g
- Cholesterol: 142 mg
- Sodium: 225 mg
- Total Carbohydrate: 62.8 g
- Protein: 23.9 g

56. Easy Roasted Vegetable Lasagna

"Roasted vegetable lasagna that I've made for years."

Serving: 10 | Prep: 35 m | Cook: 35 m | Ready in: 1 h 20 m

Ingredients

- olive oil cooking spray
- 2 zucchini, sliced
- 2 green bell peppers, cut in 1-inch pieces
- 1 (8 ounce) package sliced fresh mushrooms
- 1 onion, cut into 8 wedges
- 1 tablespoon chopped fresh basil
- 1 clove garlic, pressed
- 1/2 teaspoon salt
- 1/4 teaspoon ground black pepper
- 12 lasagna noodles
- 2 (28 ounce) jars pasta sauce
- 1 (16 ounce) package shredded mozzarella cheese
- 1 cup freshly shredded Parmesan cheese

Direction

- Preheat oven to 400 degrees F (200 degrees C). Spray a large baking sheet with cooking spray.
- Arrange zucchini, bell peppers, mushrooms, and onion wedges on prepared baking sheet. Scatter basil and garlic over vegetables and spray with cooking spray. Season with salt and black pepper.

- Bake in preheated oven until vegetables are lightly browned and tender, 10 to 25 minutes.
- Bring a large pot of lightly salted water to a boil. Cook lasagna in the boiling water, stirring occasionally until cooked through but firm to the bite, about 8 minutes. Drain.
- Bring pasta sauce to a simmer in a saucepan over medium-high heat. Mix mozzarella cheese and Parmesan cheese in a bowl.
- Pour about 1/3 cup pasta sauce in a 9x13-inch baking dish. Layer 3 lasagna noodles over sauce. Spread about of 1/4 the roasted vegetables over noodles and top with about 1/4 the sauce. Sprinkle 1/4 of the mozzarella-Parmesan cheese mixture over the sauce. Repeat layers 3 more times, ending with the cheese.
- Bake in preheated oven until cheese is melted and sauce is bubbly, 20 to 25 minutes. Allow lasagna to rest for 10 minutes before slicing.

Nutrition Information

- Calories: 410 calories
- Total Fat: 14.6 g
- Cholesterol: 38 mg
- Sodium: 1184 mg
- Total Carbohydrate: 48.4 g
- Protein: 22.2 g

57. Easy Spinach Lasagna with White Sauce

"Lasagna for the family who does not tolerate cooked tomatoes. The uncooked lasagna noodles make this recipe easy and fast. For non-vegetarians try adding a pound of sauteed hot Italian sausage. Simply delicious!"

Serving: 9

Ingredients

- 1 (10 ounce) package frozen chopped spinach
- 29 ounces Alfredo-style pasta sauce
- 1/2 cup skim milk
- 1 (8 ounce) package lasagna noodles
- 1 pint part-skim ricotta cheese
- 1 egg
- 8 ounces shredded carrots
- 8 ounces fresh mushrooms, sliced
- 1/2 cup shredded mozzarella cheese

Direction

- Preheat oven to 350 degrees F (175 degrees C). Coat a 10x15 inch lasagna pan with cooking spray.
- Place the spinach in a medium bowl. Microwave, uncovered, on high for 4 minutes. Mix in ricotta. Beat the egg with a wire whisk, and add it to the spinach and ricotta. Stir well to blend.
- Combine pasta sauce with milk in a medium bowl. Mix well.
- Spread about 1/2 cup pasta sauce mixture evenly in the bottom of the dish. Place 3 uncooked noodles over the sauce. Spread half of the spinach mixture over the noodles. Sprinkle with half

of the carrots and half of the mushrooms. Place 3 more noodles over the vegetable mixture. Pour 1 1/2 cups sauce over the noodles. Spread the remaining spinach mixture over the sauce, followed by layers of the remaining carrots and mushrooms. Place 3 more noodles over the vegetables. Pour remaining sauce evenly on top. Sprinkle with the mozzarella cheese. Spray a sheet of aluminum foil with cooking spray. Cover the dish tightly with aluminum foil, spray side down.
- Bake for 50 to 60 minutes. Remove from oven, uncover, and spoon some sauce over the exposed top noodles. Turn the oven off, and place the uncovered dish back into the warm oven for 15 more minutes. Serve at once, or let rest until ready to serve.

Nutrition Information

- Calories: 492 calories
- Total Fat: 33.7 g
- Cholesterol: 81 mg
- Sodium: 1047 mg
- Total Carbohydrate: 31.2 g
- Protein: 19.7 g

58. Easy Vegan Pasta with Kale and Chickpeas

"These is one of my go-to recipes for a quick, healthy midweek meal though it is good enough for guests, too. We eat a lot of garlic in our family, but you can of course reduce the amount."

Serving: 4 | Prep: 5 m | Cook: 17 m | Ready in: 22 m

Ingredients

- 1 (16 ounce) package spaghetti
- 1/4 cup olive oil
- 5 cloves garlic, minced
- 1 bunch kale, chopped
- 2 tablespoons nutritional yeast
- 1 (15 ounce) can chickpeas
- salt and freshly ground black pepper

Direction

- Bring a large pot of lightly salted water to a boil. Cook spaghetti in the boiling water, stirring occasionally, until tender yet firm to the bite, about 12 minutes. Drain, reserving about 1 cup of cooking water.
- Heat olive oil in a large skillet over medium heat and cook garlic until fragrant, about 1 minute. Add kale and cook, stirring constantly, until wilted, about 3 minutes.
- Stir cooked spaghetti into the skillet. Add nutritional yeast. Add enough of the reserved cooking water to create a thick sauce. Stir well. Add chickpeas and heat until warmed, 2 to 4 minutes. Season with salt and pepper.

Nutrition Information

- Calories: 692 calories
- Total Fat: 17 g
- Cholesterol: 0 mg
- Sodium: 305 mg
- Total Carbohydrate: 113.2 g
- Protein: 24 g

59. Easy Vegetarian Red Beans Lasagna

"This recipe is really easy, quick, delicious, and only requires a few ingredients."

Serving: 4 | Prep: 20 m | Cook: 35 m | Ready in: 55 m

Ingredients

- 1 tablespoon olive oil
- 1 small onion, chopped
- 1 clove garlic, minced
- 1 (15 ounce) can red beans, drained
- 1 (14.5 ounce) can diced tomatoes, drained
- 1/2 red bell pepper, chopped
- 1 teaspoon dried basil
- 1 teaspoon dried oregano
- salt and pepper to taste
- 3 tablespoons butter
- 3 tablespoons all-purpose flour
- 1 1/2 cups cold milk
- 1/2 cup grated Parmesan cheese
- 4 no-boil lasagna noodles
- 4 ounces shredded Gruyere cheese

Direction

- Preheat oven to 350 degrees F (175 degrees C).
- Heat the olive oil in a skillet over medium heat, and cook the onion until tender. Mix in garlic, and cook until heated through. Mix in red beans, tomatoes, and red bell pepper. Season with

basil, oregano, salt, and pepper. Continue cooking 10 minutes, stirring occasionally.
- Melt the butter in a saucepan over medium heat, and gradually mix in flour until smooth. Slowly stir in the milk. Mix in Parmesan cheese, and continue to cook and stir until slightly thickened.
- Spread 1/2 the red bean mixture in a 9x9 inch casserole dish, and top with 2 lasagna noodles. Layer with remaining bean mixture and remaining noodles. Cover with the sauce, and top with Gruyere cheese.
- Bake 20 minutes in the preheated oven, or until lightly browned.

Nutrition Information

- Calories: 496 calories
- Total Fat: 27 g
- Cholesterol: 71 mg
- Sodium: 800 mg
- Total Carbohydrate: 39.9 g
- Protein: 23.9 g

60. Easy Vegetarian Spaghetti with Zucchini Tomato and Feta

"This easy vegetarian spaghetti recipe with zucchini, tomatoes, garlic, and feta cheese in a cream sauce is quick to cook and so delicious that I make it almost once a week."

Serving: 4 | Prep: 15 m | Cook: 20 m | Ready in: 35 m

Ingredients

- 1 (8 ounce) package spaghetti
- 5 tomatoes
- 3 tablespoons olive oil
- 1 onion, diced
- 2 cloves garlic, minced
- 3 zucchini, cut into matchsticks
- 1 teaspoon herbes de Provence
- salt and freshly ground black pepper to taste
- 3/4 cup heavy whipping cream
- 1 tablespoon chopped fresh basil, or to taste
- 1 (8 ounce) package feta cheese, diced

Direction

- Bring a large pot of lightly salted water to a boil. Cook spaghetti in the boiling water, stirring occasionally, until tender yet firm to the bite, about 12 minutes. Drain and keep warm.
- Bring a saucepan of water to a boil while spaghetti is cooking. Cut a cross into the bottom of each tomato and place them in

the boiling water for 1 minute. Remove with a slotted spoon and immediately rinse under cold water. Peel, remove central core, and chop pulp.
- Heat olive oil in a skillet over medium heat and cook onion until soft and translucent, about 5 minutes. Add garlic and cook until fragrant, about 30 seconds. Add zucchini and cook, stirring occasionally, until softened, about 5 minutes. Season with herbes de Provence, salt, and pepper. Add tomatoes and cream and bring to a boil. Mix in basil. Stir in feta; cook until warmed through but sauce is not boiling, about 1 minute. Stir in drained spaghetti.

Nutrition Information

- Calories: 666 calories
- Total Fat: 40.2 g
- Cholesterol: 112 mg
- Sodium: 716 mg
- Total Carbohydrate: 59.4 g
- Protein: 19.8 g

61. Easy Vegetarian Spinach Lasagna

"It's easy, it's cheesy, and it's vegetarian!"

Serving: 6 | Prep: 20 m | Cook: 1 h 5 m | Ready in: 1 h 30 m

Ingredients

- cooking spray
- 9 lasagna noodles
- 1 bunch fresh spinach
- 1 (8 ounce) container ricotta cheese
- 1/2 cup shredded mozzarella cheese
- 1 egg, lightly beaten
- 1 pinch ground nutmeg
- 1 pinch dried basil
- salt and ground black pepper to taste
- 1 cup pasta sauce
- 1/2 cup shredded mozzarella cheese
- 1/4 cup grated Parmesan cheese

Direction

- Preheat oven to 400 degrees F (200 degrees C). Spray a 1 1/2-quart casserole dish with cooking spray.
- Bring a large pot of lightly salted water to a boil. Cook lasagna in the boiling water, stirring occasionally, until cooked through but firm to the bite, about 8 minutes. Drain.
- Place a steamer insert into a saucepan and fill with water to just below the bottom of the steamer. Bring water to a boil. Add

- spinach, cover, and steam until tender, 2 to 6 minutes. Drain spinach.
- Mix spinach, ricotta cheese, 1/2 cup mozzarella cheese, egg, nutmeg, basil, salt, and black pepper in a bowl until thoroughly combined.
- Spread 1/4 cup pasta sauce on the bottom of the prepared casserole dish; top with 3 lasagna noodles, 1/2 of the ricotta mixture, and 1/4 cup pasta sauce. Repeat layers of 3 more noodles, 1/2 cup ricotta mixture, and 1/4 cup pasta sauce. End with remaining 3 lasagna noodles and 1/4 cup pasta sauce. Sprinkle 1/2 cup mozzarella cheese and Parmesan cheese on top. Cover casserole with aluminum foil.
- Bake in the preheated oven for 25 minutes. Uncover casserole and continue baking until lasagna is bubbling and lightly browned, about 25 more minutes. Let lasagna stand 5 minutes before serving.

Nutrition Information

- Calories: 305 calories
- Total Fat: 10 g
- Cholesterol: 55 mg
- Sodium: 443 mg
- Total Carbohydrate: 36.8 g
- Protein: 18.3 g

62. Easy Vegetarian Stroganoff

"Fast and delicious, great over noodles, baked potato, or rice."

Serving: 7 | Prep: 5 m | Cook: 10 m | Ready in: 15 m

Ingredients

- 1 (12 ounce) package textured vegetable protein
- 2 (10.75 ounce) cans condensed cream of mushroom soup
- 1 (6 ounce) can sliced mushrooms, drained
- 2 tablespoons minced onion
- 1 tablespoon garlic powder
- 1 tablespoon seasoning salt
- 2 1/2 cups water
- 1 cup rolled oats
- 1 tablespoon olive oil

Direction

- In a large, heavy skillet over medium heat combine textured vegetable protein, mushroom soup, mushrooms, onion, garlic powder, seasoning salt, water, oats and olive oil. Stir until ingredients are well mixed, oats are moist and soup is dissolved. Reduce heat to low and simmer until thickened, about 10 minutes.

Nutrition Information

- Calories: 310 calories
- Total Fat: 9.6 g

- Cholesterol: 0 mg
- Sodium: 1541 mg
- Total Carbohydrate: 20 g
- Protein: 42.4 g

63. Eggplant Pasta

"Easy and quick pasta dish!"

Serving: 8 | Prep: 15 m | Cook: 40 m | Ready in: 55 m

Ingredients

- 1/4 cup olive oil
- 2 cloves garlic, minced
- 1 eggplant, peeled and cut into 1/2-inch cubes
- 1 (28 ounce) can plum tomatoes with juice, chopped
- 1 (16 ounce) package rigatoni pasta

Direction

- Heat olive oil in a large skillet over medium heat; cook and stir garlic until fragrant, 1 to 2 minutes. Add eggplant; cook, stirring constantly, until eggplant is softened, about 5 minutes. Add tomatoes and juice; cook until sauce is slightly reduced, about 20 minutes.
- Bring a large pot of lightly salted water to a boil. Cook rigatoni in the boiling water, stirring occasionally until cooked through but firm to the bite, about 13 minutes. Drain and transfer to a serving bowl.
- Pour sauce over pasta.

Nutrition Information

- Calories: 295 calories
- Total Fat: 8.3 g

- Cholesterol: 0 mg
- Sodium: 145 mg
- Total Carbohydrate: 48.8 g
- Protein: 8.9 g

64. Eggplant Pasta Bake

"Layers of eggplant, pasta, and a puree of vegetables called a sofrito create a dense, creamy casserole that is filling and nutritious."

Serving: 8 | Prep: 45 m | Cook: 35 m | Ready in: 1 h 20 m

Ingredients

- 1 large eggplant, peeled and thinly sliced
- 1/2 pound dry penne pasta
- 1 large onion, chopped
- 1 red bell pepper, chopped
- 2 cloves garlic
- 1 ancho chile pepper, chopped (optional)
- 2 tablespoons olive oil
- 6 tablespoons butter
- 6 tablespoons all-purpose flour
- 2 cups milk
- 1 (12 ounce) package vegetarian burger crumbles
- 1 1/2 cups shredded mozzarella cheese

Direction

- Preheat oven to 375 degrees F (190 degrees C). Lightly oil a large, deep casserole dish. Bring a large pot of lightly salted water to a boil. Add pasta and cook for 8 to 10 minutes or until al dente; drain.
- Arrange the sliced eggplant on a greased cookie sheet and bake in the preheated oven for 20 minutes.
- In a food processor, puree the onion, bell pepper, garlic and optional ancho chile pepper. If the mixture is too thick add a

tablespoon of water. In a large skillet, heat the oil over medium heat. Pour the onion mixture into the pan and cook, stirring occasionally, for 10 minutes or until the liquid has evaporated and the mixture has thickened. Remove from the heat and set aside.
- In a medium saucepan, melt butter over low heat. Stir in flour until smooth. Add milk, stirring until smooth. Remove from heat.
- Arrange half of the baked eggplant in the greased casserole dish. Spoon in half of the white sauce, covering the eggplant. Spread the veggie crumbles over the white sauce, followed by the pasta, and a layer of the bell pepper puree. Cover the onion and pepper mixture with remaining eggplant and spoon the remaining white sauce over the eggplant. Sprinkle the mozzarella cheese over the casserole.
- Bake uncovered in the preheated oven for 35 minutes. Let stand 10 minutes before serving.

Nutrition Information

- Calories: 420 calories
- Total Fat: 19.5 g
- Cholesterol: 41 mg
- Sodium: 383 mg
- Total Carbohydrate: 40.9 g
- Protein: 21 g

65. Fabulous Cilantro Pesto

"This is a delicious version of the classic with a little more zip! You can substitute the vinegar with lime juice, lemon juice or Italian salad dressing."

Serving: 8 | Prep: 15 m | Cook: 15 m | Ready in: 30 m

Ingredients

- 1 (16 ounce) package farfalle pasta
- 1 bunch fresh cilantro
- 5 cloves garlic, minced
- 1 tablespoon white wine vinegar
- 1/4 cup grated Parmesan cheese
- 1/2 teaspoon cayenne pepper
- 1/2 cup walnuts or pecans
- salt to taste
- 1/2 cup olive oil

Direction

- Bring a large pot of salted water to a boil. Add the pasta, and return water to a boil. Cook pasta for 8 to 10 minutes, or until al dente; drain well.
- In an electric food processor or blender, blend cilantro, garlic, vinegar, Parmesan cheese, cayenne pepper, nuts, and salt. Add 1/4 cup of the olive oil, and blend the pesto. Add more olive oil until the pesto reaches your desired consistency.
- Pour pesto in a small saucepan and warm over low heat, stirring constantly, until pesto begins to simmer. Pour over cooked pasta and toss.

Nutrition Information

- Calories: 386 calories
- Total Fat: 20.5 g
- Cholesterol: 3 mg
- Sodium: 55 mg
- Total Carbohydrate: 42.8 g
- Protein: 10.1 g

66. Farfalle Pasta with Zucchini and LemonCream Sauce

"Delicious and easy. A great way to use up extra zucchini."

Serving: 6 | Prep: 30 m | Cook: 25 m | Ready in: 55 m

Ingredients

- 1 (16 ounce) package farfalle (bow tie) pasta
- 1 1/2 cups whole milk ricotta cheese, at room temperature
- 1/2 cup mascarpone cheese
- 1/3 cup grated Parmesan cheese
- 2 tablespoons grated fresh lemon peel, or more to taste
- 1/4 cup chopped fresh basil
- 2 tablespoons extra-virgin olive oil
- 4 cups thinly sliced zucchini
- 6 cloves garlic, thinly sliced
- 1 teaspoon salt, divided
- 1/2 teaspoon ground black pepper, divided

Direction

- Fill a large pot with lightly salted water and bring to a rolling boil over high heat. Once the water is boiling, stir in the bow tie pasta and return to a boil. Cook the pasta uncovered, stirring occasionally, until the pasta has cooked through, but is still firm to the bite, about 12 minutes. Reserve 1/2 cup of pasta cooking water, and drain the farfalle well in a colander set in the sink.
- While the farfalle are boiling, mix together the ricotta, mascarpone, and Parmesan cheeses in a large serving bowl,

and stir in the lemon peel and basil until the mixture is well combined.
- Heat olive oil in a large skillet over medium heat, and cook and stir the zucchini and garlic until the zucchini are tender but still bright in color, about 8 minutes. Stir about 1/4 cup of the reserved pasta cooking water into the cheese mixture and mix until smooth; add the hot drained pasta and cooked zucchini, and lightly toss with the sauce. Season with the salt and pepper. If mixture is too thick, add a little more pasta cooking water, 1 tablespoon at a time, until the sauce is the desired thickness.

Nutrition Information

- Calories: 534 calories
- Total Fat: 24.3 g
- Cholesterol: 59 mg
- Sodium: 530 mg
- Total Carbohydrate: 60.6 g
- Protein: 21.2 g

67. Fettuccine Alfredo III

"Fresh pasta is the way this dish is made in the 'old country.' A simple recipe that takes about 20 minutes to prepare."

Serving: 4 | Prep: 15 m | Cook: 2 m | Ready in: 20 m

Ingredients

- 1 gallon water
- salt
- 1 pound fresh fettuccine pasta
- 1 cup butter, softened
- 1/2 cup grated Parmesan cheese
- freshly ground black pepper

Direction

- Bring the water to a rolling boil and salt to taste. Drop fresh pasta into the boiling water and cook until the noodles float to the top of the pot, 2 to 3 minutes. Drain immediately and return to the pot.
- Top with pieces of softened butter and the grated cheese; toss lightly until noodles are well coated. Season with freshly ground black pepper and serve.

Nutrition Information

- Calories: 857 calories
- Total Fat: 51.5 g
- Cholesterol: 131 mg
- Sodium: 2258 mg

- Total Carbohydrate: 83.1 g
- Protein: 19.4 g

68. Fettuccine in Creamy Mushroom and Sage Sauce

"A yummy, very quick and easy vegetarian dish. On the table in 30 minutes."

Serving: 2 | Prep: 10 m | Cook: 20 m | Ready in: 30 m

Ingredients

- 8 ounces spinach fettuccine pasta
- 1 tablespoon extra-virgin olive oil
- 1 shallot, chopped
- 1 clove garlic, chopped
- 4 ounces chopped fresh oyster mushrooms
- 1/2 cup heavy cream
- 1 tablespoon chopped fresh sage
- salt and pepper to taste

Direction

- Bring a large pot of lightly salted water to a boil. Add pasta and cook for 8 to 10 minutes, or until al dente; drain.
- Heat olive oil a medium saucepan over medium heat, and cook shallots and garlic until transparent. Stir in mushrooms, and cook until tender. Mix in heavy cream and sage. Cook and stir until thickened.
- Toss sauce with cooked fettucine, and season with salt and pepper to serve.

Nutrition Information

- Calories: 612 calories
- Total Fat: 31.4 g
- Cholesterol: 82 mg
- Sodium: 289 mg
- Total Carbohydrate: 70.2 g
- Protein: 16.5 g

69. Fettuccine Pasta with Portobello Mushrooms

"This delicious mushroom pasta dish is quick, easy, and delicious - simply ideal for a midweek supper or meat-free Monday. Serve with a salad and some garlic bread."

Serving: 3 | Prep: 10 m | Cook: 15 m | Ready in: 25 m

Ingredients

- 1 (12 ounce) box dry fettuccine pasta
- 2 tablespoons olive oil
- 1/2 onion, minced
- 1 clove garlic, minced
- 1 (8 ounce) package portobello mushrooms, thickly sliced
- 1/4 cup butter
- 3 tablespoons vegetable stock
- 1/2 bunch fresh spinach, finely chopped
- 1 sprig fresh rosemary, chopped, or to taste
- salt and freshly ground black pepper to taste
- 3 tablespoons grated Parmesan cheese

Direction

- Fill a large pot with lightly salted water and bring to a rolling boil. Cook fettuccine at a boil until tender yet firm to the bite, about 8 minutes. Drain.
- Meanwhile, heat olive oil in a skillet over medium heat and cook onion and garlic until soft, about 4 minutes. Add mushrooms and butter; cook and stir until softened, about 3 minutes. Pour in vegetable stock and cook on high heat until

stock has reduced, about 2 minutes. Add spinach and rosemary. Season with salt and pepper. Stir to combine. Add cooked linguine and toss everything to mix well. Cook for an additional 2 to 3 minutes.
- Sprinkle pasta with Parmesan cheese and mix thoroughly. Remove from heat and spoon into warmed bowls.

Nutrition Information

- Calories: 686 calories
- Total Fat: 28.8 g
- Cholesterol: 45 mg
- Sodium: 309 mg
- Total Carbohydrate: 90.8 g
- Protein: 21 g

70. Fettuccini al Fungi

"This creamy mushroom and pesto sauce is an easy dish to prepare, inspired from Seattle's Poor Italian restaurant. It is excellent for entertaining. It is best served hot from the stove!"

Serving: 6

Ingredients

- 1 pound crimini mushrooms, sliced
- 2 fresh shiitake mushrooms, stemmed and sliced
- 1 large portobello mushrooms, sliced
- 2 cloves crushed garlic
- 1/4 cup olive oil
- 2 tablespoons pesto
- 1 cup milk
- 2 tablespoons cream cheese
- 12 ounces dry fettuccine pasta

Direction

- Cook the pasta according to package directions.
- Meanwhile, sauté mushrooms and garlic in olive oil over low heat until tender. Mix in pesto mix, milk, and cream cheese; bring to a boil over medium heat. Reduce heat, and simmer while stirring until cream cheese has melted and mixture has thickened.
- Drain pasta. Pour sauce over noodles, and toss to coat. Serve.

Nutrition Information

- Calories: 377 calories
- Total Fat: 15.2 g
- Cholesterol: 10 mg
- Sodium: 105 mg
- Total Carbohydrate: 47.2 g
- Protein: 14.1 g

71. Fire and Ice Pasta

"A wonderful combination of flavors to excite even the most discerning of palates! A spicy, tomato sauce served at room temperature over hot pasta and topped with feta cheese. Goat cheese also goes well with this sauce."

Serving: 7 | Prep: 30 m | Cook: 10 m | Ready in: 3 h 40 m

Ingredients

- 2 cups olive oil
- 1/2 cup sun-dried tomatoes, sliced
- 1 (2 ounce) can sliced black olives
- 2/3 cup chopped fresh basil
- 5 1/2 pounds tomatoes, seeded and chopped
- 1/2 cup chopped fresh chives
- 1 1/2 teaspoons ground black pepper
- 1 1/2 teaspoons salt
- 1 teaspoon crushed red pepper flakes
- 4 cloves garlic, minced
- 1 (16 ounce) package farfalle pasta
- 8 ounces crumbled feta cheese (optional)

Direction

- In a large bowl, combine olive oil, sun dried tomatoes, olives, basil, tomatoes, chives, salt, black pepper, red pepper flakes, and garlic. Marinate for 3 hours.
- Cook pasta in a large pot of boiling water until al dente. Drain.
- Pour sauce over hot pasta, and toss lightly. Sprinkle with feta cheese, if desired.

Nutrition Information

- Calories: 954 calories
- Total Fat: 71.9 g
- Cholesterol: 29 mg
- Sodium: 957 mg
- Total Carbohydrate: 66.2 g
- Protein: 17.5 g

72. FireRoasted Tomato and Spinach Pasta

"DELICIOUS, cheap, fast, yet a meal you can entertain with! For a heartier meal, add some cooked chicken breast or shrimp."

Serving: 3 | Prep: 10 m | Cook: 20 m | Ready in: 30 m

Ingredients

- 6 ounces linguine pasta
- 1 tablespoon olive oil
- 3 cloves garlic, minced
- 1 (14.5 ounce) can fire-roasted diced tomatoes, with juice
- 1 (9 ounce) box frozen creamed spinach, thawed
- salt and pepper to taste

Direction

- Fill a large pot with lightly salted water and bring to a rolling boil over high heat. Once the water is boiling, stir in the linguine, and return to a boil. Cook the pasta uncovered, stirring occasionally, until the pasta has cooked through, but is still firm to the bite, about 11 minutes. Drain well in a colander set in the sink.
- Meanwhile, heat the olive oil in a large saucepan over medium heat. Stir in the garlic, and cook until softened, about 3 minutes. Stir in the fire-roasted tomatoes and bring to a simmer. Cook 1 minute before adding the creamed spinach. Cook and stir 5 minutes; season to taste with salt and pepper. Stir the drained linguine into the tomato sauce before serving.

Nutrition Information

- Calories: 349 calories
- Total Fat: 10.3 g
- Cholesterol: 24 mg
- Sodium: 802 mg
- Total Carbohydrate: 53.3 g
- Protein: 10 g

73. Flashblasted Broccoli and Feta Pasta

"The quick, high-temperature cooking method for the broccoli gives it a deep, earthy flavor. The broccoli combines with onions, garlic, feta cheese, white wine, and a splash of lemon."

Serving: 8 | Prep: 25 m | Cook: 25 m | Ready in: 50 m

Ingredients

- 1 (8 ounce) package broccoli florets
- 1 (16 ounce) package uncooked linguine pasta
- 5 tablespoons olive oil, divided
- 1/2 teaspoon salt
- 1 medium onion, chopped
- 1 clove garlic, minced
- 1/2 teaspoon crushed red pepper flakes
- 1/4 cup chopped sun-dried tomatoes (packed in oil)
- 3/4 cup dry white wine
- 1 (15 ounce) can whole peeled tomatoes, drained and chopped
- 3 cups baby spinach
- 1 1/2 tablespoons fresh lemon juice
- 4 ounces feta cheese, crumbled
- 1/4 cup pine nuts, toasted

Direction

- Preheat oven to 500 degrees F (260 degrees C). Place a baking sheet in the oven until hot.
- Place broccoli florets in a large bowl. Stir in olive oil and salt. Using oven mitts, remove the hot baking sheet from the oven.

- Pour broccoli florets onto baking sheet and spread out.
- Bake in preheated oven about 5 minutes; turn and cook about 5 minutes more. (the florets should be somewhat browned and crunchy.) Remove from oven, and set aside.
- Meanwhile, heat 2 tablespoons olive oil in a large skillet over medium heat. Stir in onions, garlic, and red pepper flakes. Cook until onion is soft and translucent. Stir in sun-dried tomatoes.
- Turn heat up to medium high. Pour in white wine, and cook about 3 minutes. Stir in chopped tomatoes. Cook about 2 minutes, then stir in spinach, lemon juice, and feta. Turn the heat down to low, and cover until pasta is done.
- While the onions are cooking, bring a large pot of lightly salted water to boil. Add linguini, and cook until al dente, about 8 to 10 minutes. Drain, and stir into broccoli mixture. Top with toasted pine nuts.

Nutrition Information

- Calories: 393 calories
- Total Fat: 15.7 g
- Cholesterol: 13 mg
- Sodium: 417 mg
- Total Carbohydrate: 49.7 g
- Protein: 12.6 g

74. Four Cheese Macaroni and Cheese

"This is a layered four cheese recipe that my very good friend gave me. She knew I didn't like to cook and this was pretty simple to do. Now I make this dish every Thanksgiving."

Serving: 9 | Prep: 20 m | Cook: 20 m | Ready in: 40 m

Ingredients

- 1/2 (8 ounce) package elbow macaroni
- 1 cup shredded sharp Cheddar cheese
- 1 cup shredded provolone cheese
- 1 cup shredded mozzarella cheese
- 1 cup shredded Colby-Monterey Jack cheese
- 1 egg, beaten
- 1 cup milk

Direction

- Bring a large saucepan of lightly salted water to a boil. Place macaroni in the saucepan and cook for 8 to 10 minutes, or until al dente; drain.
- Preheat oven to 350 degrees F (175 degrees C). Lightly grease an 8x8 inch baking dish.
- Spread the Cheddar cheese over the bottom of the baking dish. Top with a thin layer of macaroni. Top macaroni with Provolone cheese, another layer of macaroni, a layer of mozzarella and a third layer of macaroni. Top with a layer of Colby-Monterey Jack cheese. Pour the egg over all, followed by the milk.

- Bake in the preheated oven 20 minutes, or until bubbly and golden brown.

Nutrition Information

- Calories: 260 calories
- Total Fat: 16.2 g
- Cholesterol: 69 mg
- Sodium: 420 mg
- Total Carbohydrate: 11.9 g
- Protein: 16.5 g

75. Four Cheese Macaroni Casserole

"This casserole is quick and easy but full of flavor. Both children and adults love it!"

Serving: 6 | Prep: 20 m | Cook: 40 m | Ready in: 1 h

Ingredients

- 3 cups uncooked macaroni
- 1 (28 ounce) can whole peeled tomatoes, drained and chopped
- 1 teaspoon Italian seasoning
- 1 teaspoon dried oregano
- 1 teaspoon basil
- salt and pepper to taste
- 1 1/2 cups grated Cheddar cheese
- 1 1/2 cups shredded mozzarella cheese
- 3/4 cup freshly grated Parmesan cheese
- 1/4 cup crumbled feta cheese

Direction

- Preheat oven to 350 degrees F (175 degrees C).
- Bring a large pot of lightly salted water to boil over high heat. Add macaroni, and cook until al dente, about 8 to 10 minutes. Drain, and pour hot pasta into a casserole dish.
- Meanwhile, in a large bowl, stir together tomatoes, Italian seasoning, oregano, basil, salt, and pepper.
- Stir into the hot pasta 1 cup of Cheddar, 1 cup of mozzarella, and 1/2 cup of Parmesan. Continue to stir until the cheeses

have melted. Then stir in tomato and herb mixture. Sprinkle 1/2 cup Cheddar, 1/2 cup mozzarella, 1/4 cup Parmesan, and 1/4 cup feta over the top of the casserole.
- Bake in preheated oven for 15 to 25 minutes.

Nutrition Information

- Calories: 511 calories
- Total Fat: 22.8 g
- Cholesterol: 75 mg
- Sodium: 887 mg
- Total Carbohydrate: 47 g
- Protein: 29.7 g

76. Fresh Tomato Pasta

"This is an extremely simple pasta recipe that I love to make when I don't really feel like cooking! I use rigatoni, but you can use whatever pasta you prefer. This is especially delicious with tomatoes fresh from your garden. Serve with garlic bread and a simple lettuce salad with Italian dressing."

Serving: 2 | Prep: 10 m | Cook: 12 m | Ready in: 22 m

Ingredients

- 1 (8 ounce) package dry pasta
- 1 clove garlic
- 1 medium tomato
- 1 teaspoon dried basil
- 1 tablespoon olive oil
- 1 pinch salt

Direction

- Fill a large pot with lightly salted water and bring to a rolling boil over high heat.
- Coarsely chop the tomato and transfer to a small bowl. Sprinkle the tomato chunks with basil, olive oil, and salt. Set aside.
- Once the water is boiling, stir in the rigatoni, and return to a boil. Cook the pasta uncovered, stirring occasionally, until the pasta has cooked through, but is still firm to the bite, about 12 minutes. Drain well in a colander, and then return the pasta to the pot.
- Pour the tomato mixture over the pasta and toss to mix.

Nutrition Information

- Calories: 501 calories
- Total Fat: 12 g
- Cholesterol: 134 mg
- Sodium: 33 mg
- Total Carbohydrate: 82.2 g
- Protein: 17.1 g

77. Fusilli with Rapini Broccoli Rabe Garlic and Tomato Wine Sauce

"Delicious in the spring, cut rapini before it flowers for tender greenery. Absolutely delicious and very easily adaptable for whatever's growing in your garden."

Serving: 2 | Prep: 20 m | Cook: 20 m | Ready in: 40 m

Ingredients

- 1 bunch broccoli rabe, trimmed and cut into 1-inch pieces
- 1/2 cup uncooked fusilli pasta
- 3 tablespoons olive oil
- 2 cloves garlic, roughly chopped
- salt and ground black pepper to taste
- 1 sprig fresh rosemary (optional)
- 1/2 teaspoon dried Italian herb mix, or to taste
- 1/4 teaspoon crushed red pepper flakes, or to taste
- 1/4 cup white wine
- 1 (14.5 ounce) can diced tomatoes
- 2 green onions, sliced
- 1 clove garlic, minced
- 2 teaspoons grated Parmesan cheese, or to taste

Direction

- Fill a saucepan with enough water to cover the broccoli rabe, sprinkle in some salt, and bring the salted water to a boil. Stir in the broccoli rabe, and cook until bright green and just starting to become tender, about 2 minutes; drain the rabe, and cool in

a bowl of ice water to stop the cooking process. Drain well, and pat dry with paper towels.
- Fill a pot with lightly salted water and bring to a rolling boil over high heat. Once the water is boiling, stir in the fusilli, and return to a boil. Cook the pasta uncovered, stirring occasionally, until the pasta has cooked through, but is still firm to the bite, about 12 minutes. Drain well in a colander set in the sink.
- While the pasta is cooking, heat the olive oil in a saucepan over medium heat, and cook and stir the 2 roughly-chopped garlic cloves until they start to turn translucent, about 2 minutes; sprinkle with salt and black pepper, and stir in rosemary sprig, dried Italian herb mix, and crushed red pepper flakes.
- Stir in the blanched rabe, white wine, and tomatoes; remove rosemary sprig, and bring the mixture to a boil. Mix in the cooked fusilli pasta, green onions, and 1 minced clove of garlic; simmer for 1 more minute, and serve topped with a sprinkle of Parmesan cheese.

Nutrition Information

- Calories: 353 calories
- Total Fat: 21.3 g
- Cholesterol: 2 mg
- Sodium: 390 mg
- Total Carbohydrate: 26.3 g
- Protein: 9 g

78. Game Day Mac and Mex

"This south-of-the-border spin on mac and cheese anchors any game day spread like a strong offensive line and adds real weight to a game day plate. Can garnish with sour cream, hot sauce, more cilantro or more salsa."

Serving: 12 | Prep: 20 m | Cook: 45 m | Ready in: 1 h 15 m

Ingredients

- 1 (16 ounce) package elbow macaroni
- 1/2 cup butter, divided
- 1/2 cup all-purpose flour
- 1 quart milk, warmed
- 1 tablespoon salt
- 1 teaspoon ground white pepper
- 1 teaspoon ground nutmeg
- 6 cups shredded Mexican-style 4-cheese blend (such as Sargento®)
- 1 (15 ounce) can black beans, rinsed and drained
- 2 avocados, chopped
- 2 (4 ounce) cans chopped green chiles
- 1 cup chopped green onions
- 2 tablespoons chopped fresh cilantro
- 2 cups salsa

Direction

- Preheat oven to 375 degrees F (190 degrees C).
- Bring a large pot of lightly salted water to a boil. Cook elbow macaroni in the boiling water, stirring occasionally, until cooked

through but firm to the bite, 6 to 7 minutes. Drain and transfer to a large mixing bowl; stir in 2 tablespoons butter until coated.
- Melt remaining 6 tablespoons butter in a large skillet over medium heat; whisk flour into melted butter. Cook, stirring constantly, until mixture is lightly golden and smooth. Slowly whisk warm milk into flour mixture until smooth. Whisk salt, white pepper, and nutmeg into white sauce, bring to a simmer, and whisk until smooth and thickened, about 3 minutes. Remove sauce from heat and gradually stir Mexican-style cheese into sauce until melted and thick.
- Pour cheese sauce over macaroni and gently fold black beans, avocados, green chiles, green onions, and cilantro into the macaroni mixture. Transfer to a 9x13-inch glass baking dish. Spoon salsa over the casserole in decorative swirls or lines.
- Bake in the preheated oven until the top has begun to brown and the casserole is bubbling, 30 to 45 minutes. Let the casserole rest about 10 minutes before serving.

Nutrition Information

- Calories: 572 calories
- Total Fat: 31.1 g
- Cholesterol: 77 mg
- Sodium: 1629 mg
- Total Carbohydrate: 50.9 g
- Protein: 24 g

79. Garage Noodles

"A quick ramen noodle dish with kale and mushrooms that is ready in 25 minutes. If you have cooked shrimp or chicken, you can add those in as well. Bon appetit!"

Serving: 4 | Prep: 10 m | Cook: 15 m | Ready in: 25 m

Ingredients

- 4 (3 ounce) packages ramen noodles (without flavor packet)
- 1 tablespoon vegetable oil
- 2 medium onions, cut into thin wedges
- 1 (6 ounce) package sliced fresh mushrooms
- 1 small bunch Tuscan kale, stemmed and chopped
- kosher salt
- 1/2 cup rice vinegar
- 1/3 cup soy sauce
- 1 teaspoon sesame oil

Direction

- Bring a pot of water to a boil. Add ramen and cook, stirring occasionally, until soft, about 3 minutes. Drain, saving 1/2 cup of cooking liquid.
- Heat oil in a large skillet over medium heat and cook onions until softened, 3 to 5 minutes. Add drained ramen, mushrooms, kale, and salt. Add some of the cooking liquid, rice vinegar, soy sauce, and sesame oil and cook until kale has wilted and mushrooms are soft, about 5 minutes.

Nutrition Information

- Calories: 490 calories
- Total Fat: 19.5 g
- Cholesterol: 0 mg
- Sodium: 1727 mg
- Total Carbohydrate: 67.5 g
- Protein: 14.4 g

80. Garlicky Vodka Alfredo

"Garlic with a hint of vodka. What's not to love?"

Serving: 4 | Prep: 10 m | Cook: 15 m | Ready in: 25 m

Ingredients

- 1 (16 ounce) package penne rigate
- 1 tablespoon extra-virgin olive oil
- 7 cloves roasted garlic
- 1/2 cup butter
- 1 1/2 cups heavy cream
- 1/4 cup chicken stock
- 1/2 cup vodka
- 2 cups grated Parmesan cheese
- 1/2 cup grated Asiago cheese
- kosher salt to taste
- ground white pepper to taste
- 10 leaves fresh basil, torn or shredded

Direction

- Bring a large pot of lightly-salted water to a boil. Add pasta and cook until al dente, 8 to 10 minutes; drain.
- Heat the oil in a large skillet over medium heat; cook the garlic in the oil about 3 minutes. Stir in the butter, cream, chicken stock, and vodka; bring to a simmer. Add the Parmesan cheese, Asiago cheese, salt, and pepper; stir. Mix the pasta into the sauce and stir to coat. Allow to simmer about 3 minutes more. Garnish with fresh basil to serve.

Nutrition Information

- Calories: 1284 calories
- Total Fat: 80.2 g
- Cholesterol: 239 mg
- Sodium: 1276 mg
- Total Carbohydrate: 88.1 g
- Protein: 40 g

81. Ginas Creamy Mushroom Lasagna

"If you like mushrooms, then this recipe is right up your alley. It's great to make for dinner or entertaining."

Serving: 8 | Prep: 30 m | Cook: 55 m | Ready in: 1 h 35 m

Ingredients

- 12 uncooked lasagna noodles
- cooking spray
- 1 tablespoon olive oil
- 1 cup chopped shallots
- 2 garlic cloves, minced
- 1 cup diced red bell pepper
- 1 teaspoon crushed red pepper flakes
- 4 cups sliced fresh mushrooms
- salt and ground black pepper to taste
- 1 1/2 cups ricotta cheese
- 1/4 cup butter
- 2 tablespoons all-purpose flour
- 4 cups milk
- 1 cup grated Parmesan cheese
- 1 cup shredded mozzarella cheese
- 1/4 cup chopped fresh flat-leaf parsley

Direction

- Bring a large pot of lightly salted water to a boil. Stir in lasagna noodles and return to a boil. Cook the pasta uncovered, stirring

- occasionally, until the noodles have cooked through but are still firm to the bite, about 8 minutes. Drain and set aside.
- Preheat oven to 350 degrees F (175 degrees C).
- Spray a 9x13-inch baking dish with cooking spray.
- Heat olive oil in a large skillet over medium-high heat. Cook and stir shallots and garlic in the hot oil until shallots are tender and translucent, about 5 minutes.
- Stir red bell pepper and red pepper flakes into the shallot mixture until bell pepper is slightly softened, 1 to 2 minutes.
- Mix mushrooms into the skillet; season with salt and black pepper. Cook and stir until the mushrooms have given up their liquid and are browned, about 10 minutes more.
- Stir ricotta cheese into the mushroom mixture; remove skillet from heat and set aside.
- Melt butter in another skillet over medium heat. Whisk in flour until smooth, 2 to 3 minutes.
- Whisk milk into flour mixture until smooth; bring to a simmer and whisk constantly until thickened, about 5 minutes. Season with salt and black pepper.
- Coat the bottom of the prepared baking dish with a small amount of the white sauce.
- Arrange 4 lasagna noodles in a single layer over the white sauce.
- Spread about 1/3 of the mushroom mixture over the noodles.
- Pour about 1/3 of the white sauce over the mushroom mixture. Repeat the layers 2 more times, starting with 4 more lasagna noodles.
- Sprinkle Parmesan cheese, mozzarella cheese, and parsley over the lasagna.
- Bake in the preheated oven until cheese is melted and sauce is bubbly, 30 to 40 minutes. Allow lasagna to rest for 10 minutes before slicing and serving.

Nutrition Information

- Calories: 371 calories
- Total Fat: 16 g
- Cholesterol: 41 mg
- Sodium: 356 mg
- Total Carbohydrate: 40.3 g
- Protein: 18.2 g

82. Gnocchi and Peppers in Balsamic Sauce

"This is a great twist on gnocchi! Garlic, basil, onion, mushrooms, sweet peppers, and tomatoes are sauteed before mixing with butter and balsamic vinegar to make a sauce."

Serving: 4 | Prep: 30 m | Cook: 30 m | Ready in: 1 h

Ingredients

- 2 tablespoons olive oil
- 3 cloves garlic, chopped
- 1/2 cup diced red onion
- salt to taste
- 6 crimini mushrooms, chopped
- 4 small mixed sweet peppers, julienned
- 1/2 cup cherry tomatoes, halved
- 4 leaves fresh basil, chopped
- 1/2 cup balsamic vinegar
- 1 (16 ounce) package potato gnocchi
- 1 cup Additional butter or margarine

Direction

- Cook the gnocchi according to package directions; drain.
- Heat the olive oil in a skillet over medium heat. Add garlic to the skillet and cook for 2 minutes. Mix in the chopped onions and season with salt; cook until onions begin to soften, about 5 minutes. Stir in the mushrooms, peppers, tomatoes, and basil; cook for another 5 minutes. Stir the butter in to melt. Pour the balsamic vinegar into the skillet, stir, reduce heat, and simmer

the sauce for 15 to 20 minutes. Toss the cooked gnocchi with the sauce.

Nutrition Information

- Calories: 693 calories
- Total Fat: 61 g
- Cholesterol: 143 mg
- Sodium: 435 mg
- Total Carbohydrate: 33.8 g
- Protein: 5.9 g

83. Gnocchi I

"This simple potato, flour, and egg recipe is one my family has used for generations."

Serving: 4 | Prep: 30 m | Cook: 30 m | Ready in: 1 h

Ingredients

- 2 potatoes
- 2 cups all-purpose flour
- 1 egg

Direction

- Bring a large pot of salted water to a boil. Peel potatoes and add to pot. Cook until tender but still firm, about 15 minutes. Drain, cool and mash with a fork or potato masher.
- Combine 1 cup mashed potato, flour and egg in a large bowl. Knead until dough forms a ball. Shape small portions of the dough into long "snakes". On a floured surface, cut snakes into half-inch pieces.
- Bring a large pot of lightly salted water to a boil. Drop in gnocchi and cook for 3 to 5 minutes or until gnocchi have risen to the top; drain and serve.

Nutrition Information

- Calories: 329 calories
- Total Fat: 2 g
- Cholesterol: 53 mg
- Sodium: 22 mg

- Total Carbohydrate: 67 g
- Protein: 9.7 g

84. Gnocchi Primavera

"Potato gnocchi with wonderful crisp vegetables and basil make a delicious, rustic meal."

Serving: 4 | Prep: 10 m | Cook: 20 m | Ready in: 30 m

Ingredients

- 1/2 cup freshly grated Parmesan cheese, divided
- 1 teaspoon olive oil
- 2 tablespoons pine nuts
- 1 (16 ounce) package potato gnocchi
- 2 tablespoons olive oil, divided
- 1 zucchini, chopped
- 12 fresh mushrooms, cleaned and stems trimmed
- 12 grape tomatoes
- 10 torn fresh basil leaves

Direction

- Spray a nonstick skillet with cooking spray, and place over medium-low heat. Place about 2 tablespoons of Parmesan cheese at a time into the skillet. Cook until the cheese melts into a thin circle, begins to bubble, and browns at the edges, about 1 minute. Flip the crisp, and brown the other side for about 30 seconds. Remove the crisp to a plate to cool. Make 3 more cheese crisps the same way.
- Heat 1 teaspoon of olive oil in a skillet over medium heat, and cook and stir the pine nuts until lightly toasted and fragrant, about 3 minutes. Remove the pine nuts from the skillet and set aside.

- Cook the gnocchi according to the package directions, and drain them in a colander set in the sink.
- Pour 1 tablespoon of olive oil in a large skillet over high heat, and cook and stir the zucchini just until seared, about 2 minutes; remove the zucchini from the pan. Reduce the heat to medium, and cook and stir the mushrooms in the same pan, until they begin to give up their juices but are still firm, about 5 minutes. Drain the juices. Return the zucchini to the pan; add the tomatoes, torn basil leaves, toasted pine nuts, drained gnocchi, and the remaining 1 tablespoon olive oil, and stir a few times to combine and heat through.
- To serve, divide gnocchi among four plates, and serve each plate topped with a Parmesan cheese crisp.

Nutrition Information

- Calories: 327 calories
- Total Fat: 21.3 g
- Cholesterol: 30 mg
- Sodium: 249 mg
- Total Carbohydrate: 26.2 g
- Protein: 10.2 g

85. Gorgonzola Cream Sauce

"Autumn is the season for rich, creamy sauces, and I'm pretty sure you're going to be shocked at just how easy this one is. When your cream is reduced, your sauce is practically done. I like serving this with a stuffed pasta like tortellini or ravioli, topped with diced apple and crunchy toasted walnuts."

Serving: 6 | Prep: 15 m | Cook: 25 m | Ready in: 40 m

Ingredients

- 1 cup heavy whipping cream
- salt and freshly ground black pepper to taste
- 1 pinch cayenne pepper, or to taste
- 6 ounces dry miniature ravioli
- 3 ounces crumbled Gorgonzola cheese
- 2 tablespoons chopped Italian flat leaf parsley
- 2 tablespoons freshly grated Parmesan cheese
- 1/2 apple, diced
- 1/4 cup chopped toasted walnuts
- 1 teaspoon chopped Italian flat leaf parsley

Direction

- Place a heavy skillet over medium heat. Pour cream into skillet, bring to a simmer, and cook cream until it reduces by half, about 8 minutes, stirring occasionally. Season with salt, black pepper, and cayenne pepper.
- Bring a pot of salted water to a boil. Pour dried ravioli into boiling water and cook, stirring occasionally, until pasta is tender, 16 to 18 minutes. Drain pasta, reserving a cup of pasta water.

- Gently fold cooked ravioli into cream sauce and turn heat to low. Mix in Gorgonzola cheese, stirring gently until melted. If sauce is too thick, thin it with a little pasta cooking water.
- Stir in 2 tablespoons parsley and Parmesan cheese. Transfer to a serving bowl and sprinkle with diced apple, walnuts, and 1 teaspoon parsley.

Nutrition Information

- Calories: 300 calories
- Total Fat: 24.4 g
- Cholesterol: 82 mg
- Sodium: 258 mg
- Total Carbohydrate: 12.6 g
- Protein: 8.5 g

86. Grandmas Gnocchi

"My grandmother used to make these when I was a little girl. When I was old enough to realize that I needed to get her delicious recipes, she showed me how to make a lot of her wonderful dishes. She never wrote anything down and she rarely used a cookbook. She also didn't measure things the same each time, so sometimes you have to add a little to the recipes."

Serving: 8 | Prep: 15 m | Cook: 20 m | Ready in: 35 m

Ingredients

- 6 russet potatoes
- 1 cup all-purpose flour
- 1 egg, lightly beaten
- 1 tablespoon olive oil
- 1 pinch salt

Direction

- Bring a large pot of salted water to a boil. Drop in potatoes and cook until tender but still firm, about 15 minutes. Drain, cool slightly, and peel. Season with salt, then mash potatoes with fork, masher, or in ricer. Place in large bowl, and stir in egg and olive oil. Knead in enough flour to make a soft dough.
- On a floured surface, roll dough into a long rope. Cut the rope into 1/2-inch pieces.
- Bring a large pot of lightly salted water to a boil. Drop in gnocchi, and cook until they float to the top, about 3 to 5 minutes. Serve with pasta sauce.

Nutrition Information

- Calories: 204 calories
- Total Fat: 2.6 g
- Cholesterol: 23 mg
- Sodium: 19 mg
- Total Carbohydrate: 39.9 g
- Protein: 5.6 g

87. Greek Fettuccine

"Spinach fettuccine is served with a quick sauce of tomatoes and feta cheese."

Serving: 4 | Prep: 15 m | Cook: 10 m | Ready in: 25 m

Ingredients

- 1 (16 ounce) package spinach fettuccine pasta
- 1 1/2 cups chopped fresh tomatoes
- 1 tablespoon chopped fresh mint
- 1/4 cup chopped black olives (optional)
- 3/4 cup crumbled feta cheese
- 1 pinch salt and ground black pepper to taste

Direction

- Fill a large pot with lightly salted water and bring to a rolling boil over high heat. Once the water is boiling, stir in the fettuccine, and return to a boil. Cook the pasta uncovered, stirring occasionally, until the pasta has cooked through, but is still firm to the bite, about 8 minutes. Drain well in a colander set in the sink.
- Place the tomatoes, mint, and black olives (if using) into a saucepan over medium-low heat, and bring to a bare simmer. Stir in the feta cheese, and allow to melt slightly.
- Place the spinach fettuccine into a serving bowl, and toss with the tomato mixture. Season to taste with salt and black pepper.

Nutrition Information

- Calories: 401 calories
- Total Fat: 9.5 g
- Cholesterol: 25 mg
- Sodium: 651 mg
- Total Carbohydrate: 65.2 g
- Protein: 17.5 g

88. Greek God Pasta

"Delicious, quick and easy, fit for a god! One can substitute Parmesan cheese for feta cheese. Serve with a Greek salad or bruschetta"

Serving: 6 | Prep: 20 m | Cook: 30 m | Ready in: 50 m

Ingredients

- 1 (16 ounce) package whole wheat rotini pasta
- 1 (16 ounce) can peeled and diced tomatoes, drained
- 2 tablespoons chopped green bell pepper
- 1/4 cup chopped green onion
- 3 cups tomato sauce
- 1 teaspoon dried basil
- 1 teaspoon dried oregano
- 1 cup sliced black olives
- 1/2 cup shredded mozzarella cheese
- 2 tablespoons crumbled feta cheese

Direction

- Preheat the oven to 400 degrees F (200 degrees C).
- Bring a large pot of lightly salted water to a boil. Add rotini pasta, and cook until al dente, about 8 minutes. Drain and pour into a deep casserole dish.
- Stir tomatoes, green pepper, green onion, olives and tomato sauce into the pasta. Season with basil and oregano and mix until evenly blended. Sprinkle mozzarella and feta cheese over the top.
- Bake for 30 minutes in the preheated oven, until cheese is melted and bubbly. Let stand for a few minutes before serving.

Nutrition Information

- Calories: 371 calories
- Total Fat: 6 g
- Cholesterol: 9 mg
- Sodium: 1068 mg
- Total Carbohydrate: 68.5 g
- Protein: 16.4 g

89. Greek Orzo with Feta

"This recipe has easy ingredients and is a great light lunch or dinner! Enjoy!"

Serving: 6 | Prep: 30 m | Cook: 10 m | Ready in: 1 h 40 m

Ingredients

- 1/4 cup olive oil
- 1/2 cup fresh lemon juice
- 1/2 cup pitted kalamata olives, chopped
- 2 ripe tomatoes, seeded and diced
- 1 red bell pepper, chopped
- 1 red onion, chopped
- 2 cloves garlic, minced
- 1 teaspoon finely chopped fresh oregano
- 1 (8 ounce) package crumbled feta cheese
- 1/2 pound dried orzo pasta
- 1 cup chopped fresh parsley

Direction

- Stir together olive oil, lemon juice, olives, tomatoes, red pepper, red onion, garlic, oregano, and feta cheese in a large bowl. Let stand at room temperature for 1 hour.
- Bring a large pot of lightly salted water to a boil. Add the orzo and cook for 8 to 10 minutes or until al dente; drain and toss the tomato mixture. Sprinkle with chopped parsley to serve.

Nutrition Information

- Calories: 381 calories
- Total Fat: 20.8 g
- Cholesterol: 34 mg
- Sodium: 618 mg
- Total Carbohydrate: 38.4 g
- Protein: 12 g

90. Greek Pasta with Tomatoes and White Beans

"An easy, quick, and tasty recipe. The flavors are wonderfully different as they are combined and meld together."

Serving: 4 | Prep: 10 m | Cook: 15 m | Ready in: 25 m

Ingredients

- 2 (14.5 ounce) cans Italian-style diced tomatoes
- 1 (19 ounce) can cannellini beans, drained and rinsed
- 10 ounces fresh spinach, washed and chopped
- 8 ounces penne pasta
- 1/2 cup crumbled feta cheese

Direction

- Cook the pasta in a large pot of boiling salted water until al dente.
- Meanwhile, combine tomatoes and beans in a large non-stick skillet. Bring to a boil over medium high heat. Reduce heat, and simmer 10 minutes.
- Add spinach to the sauce; cook for 2 minutes or until spinach wilts, stirring constantly.
- Serve sauce over pasta, and sprinkle with feta.

Nutrition Information

- Calories: 460 calories
- Total Fat: 5.9 g

- Cholesterol: 17 mg
- Sodium: 593 mg
- Total Carbohydrate: 79 g
- Protein: 23.4 g

91. Greek Spaghetti II

"Just like YaYa used to make!! The trick is to not over-burn the butter!"

Serving: 4 | Prep: 5 m | Cook: 25 m | Ready in: 30 m

Ingredients

- 1 pound spaghetti
- 6 tablespoons butter
- 1/2 teaspoon salt
- 1 cup grated Parmesan cheese
- 1 teaspoon dried oregano

Direction

- Preheat oven to 250 degrees F (120 degrees C).
- Bring a large pot of lightly salted water to a boil. Add pasta and cook for 8 to 10 minutes or until al dente; drain.
- In a medium skillet over medium heat, melt butter with salt and cook until just brown. Remove from heat and toss with pasta, cheese and oregano. Pour into a 7x11 inch baking dish.
- Bake in preheated oven 10 to 15 minutes, until hot and bubbly.

Nutrition Information

- Calories: 661 calories
- Total Fat: 24.8 g
- Cholesterol: 63 mg
- Sodium: 726 mg
- Total Carbohydrate: 85.8 g

- Protein: 22.7 g

92. Green Green Pasta

"Light and quick pasta dish using fresh summer vegetables."

Serving: 4 | Prep: 15 m | Cook: 30 m | Ready in: 45 m

Ingredients

- 1 (8 ounce) package pappardelle pasta
- 2 tablespoons olive oil, divided
- 1 zucchini, halved and sliced
- 1 bunch thin asparagus, cut into 1 1/2-inch lengths
- 1 crown broccoli, cut into florets
- 8 ounces fresh green beans, cut into 1-inch lengths
- 2 green onions, thinly sliced
- 1 (15 ounce) can garbanzo beans, drained and rinsed
- 2 tablespoons reserved pasta water
- 1 tablespoon chopped fresh basil
- salt and pepper to taste
- 1/4 cup crumbled feta cheese

Direction

- Bring a large pot of lightly salted water to boil. Add pappardelle, and cook until al dente, 8 to 10 minutes. Drain, reserving some pasta water. Coat with 1 tablespoon olive oil; set aside.
- Meanwhile, heat 1 tablespoon olive oil in a large non-stick skillet over medium high heat. Add zucchini; cook and stir until zucchini begins to brown around the edges but is still firm. Stir in asparagus, broccoli, and green beans; continue to cook until vegetables turn bright green in color, about 3 minutes. Add

green onions and garbanzo beans; cook and stir until vegetables are lightly browned around the edges.
- Add reserved pasta water to vegetables. Cover skillet; reduce heat to low and simmer until garbanzos are heated through and vegetables are just tender. Stir vegetables and basil into pasta; season to taste with salt and pepper, and top with crumbled feta.

Nutrition Information

- Calories: 429 calories
- Total Fat: 10.9 g
- Cholesterol: 8 mg
- Sodium: 340 mg
- Total Carbohydrate: 69.1 g
- Protein: 16.8 g

93. Hearty Vegetable Lasagna

"This hearty, vegetable lasagna is the only lasagna my husband will eat. We love it!!! Hope you all enjoy as much as we do."

Serving: 12 | Prep: 25 m | Cook: 1 h | Ready in: 1 h 40 m

Ingredients

- 1 (16 ounce) package lasagna noodles
- 1 pound fresh mushrooms, sliced
- 3/4 cup chopped green bell pepper
- 3/4 cup chopped onion
- 3 cloves garlic, minced
- 2 tablespoons vegetable oil
- 2 (26 ounce) jars pasta sauce
- 1 teaspoon dried basil
- 1 (15 ounce) container part-skim ricotta cheese
- 4 cups shredded mozzarella cheese
- 2 eggs
- 1/2 cup grated Parmesan cheese

Direction

- Cook the lasagna noodles in a large pot of boiling water for 10 minutes, or until al dente. Rinse with cold water, and drain.
- In a large saucepan, cook and stir mushrooms, green peppers, onion, and garlic in oil. Stir in pasta sauce and basil; bring to a boil. Reduce heat, and simmer 15 minutes.
- Mix together ricotta, 2 cups mozzarella cheese, and eggs.
- Preheat oven to 350 degrees F (175 degrees C). Spread 1 cup tomato sauce into the bottom of a greased 9x13 inch baking

dish. Layer 1/2 each, lasagna noodles, ricotta mix, sauce, and Parmesan cheese. Repeat layering, and top with remaining 2 cups mozzarella cheese.
- Bake, uncovered, for 40 minutes. Let stand 15 minutes before serving.

Nutrition Information

- Calories: 462 calories
- Total Fat: 19.5 g
- Cholesterol: 77 mg
- Sodium: 843 mg
- Total Carbohydrate: 49.6 g
- Protein: 23.2 g

94. Homemade Four Cheese Ravioli

"Great homemade Italian ravioli recipe that I have recreated to taste like the ravioli at Maggiano's restaurant. Don't be intimidated by the large list of ingredients, it is well worth it!"

Serving: 4 | Prep: 45 m | Cook: 15 m | Ready in: 2 h

Ingredients

- Ravioli Dough:
- 2 cups all-purpose flour
- 1 pinch salt
- 1 teaspoon olive oil
- 2 eggs
- 1 1/2 tablespoons water
- Ravioli Filling:
- 1 (8 ounce) container ricotta cheese
- 1 (4 ounce) package cream cheese, softened
- 1/2 cup shredded mozzarella cheese
- 1/2 cup provolone cheese, shredded
- 1 egg
- 1 1/2 teaspoons dried parsley
- Pesto-Alfredo Cream Sauce:
- 2 tablespoons olive oil
- 2 cloves garlic, crushed
- 3 tablespoons prepared basil pesto sauce
- 2 cups heavy cream
- 1/4 cup grated Parmesan cheese
- 1 (24 ounce) jar marinara sauce
- Egg Wash:

- 1 egg
- 1 tablespoon water

Direction

- Mound the flour and salt together on a work surface and form a well. Beat the teaspoon of olive oil, 2 eggs, and water in a bowl. Pour half the egg mixture into the well. Begin mixing the egg with the flour with one hand; use your other hand to keep the flour mound steady. Add the remaining egg mixture and knead to form a dough.
- Knead the dough until smooth, 8 to 10 minutes; add more flour if the dough is too sticky. Form the dough into a ball and wrap tightly with plastic. Refrigerate for 1 hour.
- While the dough is resting, prepare the ravioli filling. Combine the ricotta cheese, cream cheese, mozzarella cheese, provolone cheese, egg, and parsley and mix well. Set the filling aside.
- Heat 2 tablespoons of olive oil in a skillet over medium heat. Add the crushed garlic and pesto sauce and cook for one minute. Pour in the heavy cream, raise the heat to high, and bring the sauce to a boil. Reduce the heat and simmer for 5 minutes. Add the Parmesan cheese and stir until the cheese melts. Remove the pan from the heat and keep warm.
- Meanwhile, in a separate saucepan, warm the marinara sauce over medium-low heat.
- Preheat an oven to 375 degrees F (190 degrees C). Beat the egg with the tablespoon of water to make the egg wash.
- Roll out the pasta dough into thin sheets no thicker than a nickel. To assemble the ravioli, brush the egg wash over a sheet of pasta. Drop the filling mixture on the dough by teaspoonfuls about one inch apart. Cover the filling with the top sheet of pasta, pressing out the air from around each portion of

filling. Press firmly around the filling to seal. Cut into individual ravioli with a knife or pizza cutter. Seal the edges.
- Fill a large pot with lightly salted water and bring to a rolling boil over high heat. Stir in the ravioli, and return to a boil. Cook uncovered, stirring occasionally, until the ravioli float to the top and the filling is hot, 4 to 8 minutes. Drain well.
- Grease a baking sheet. Place the cooked ravioli on the sheet pan and bake in the preheated oven until brown, about 4 minutes.
- To serve the ravioli, divide them among four warmed serving bowls. Drizzle the marinara sauce over the ravioli and then top with the cream sauce.

Nutrition Information

- Calories: 1270 calories
- Total Fat: 89.2 g
- Cholesterol: 407 mg
- Sodium: 1359 mg
- Total Carbohydrate: 80.4 g
- Protein: 37.8 g

95. Homemade GlutenFree and LactoseFree Vegetable Lasagna

"Homemade vegetable lasagna just as it should be; hot, oozy, and messy! This is a vegetable lasagna without any weird micro-protein meat substitute; just vegetables and tomatoes, with a homemade white sauce (made with lactose-free milk and cheese, and gluten-free flour). I have been known to make my own pasta sheets for this, but tonight I used Sainsbury's gluten-free pasta sheets (dry)."

Serving: 8 | Prep: 40 m | Cook: 1 h 10 m | Ready in: 2 h 5 m

Ingredients

- 1 tablespoon vegetable oil, or as needed
- 2 small onion, chopped
- 1 red bell pepper, chopped
- 2 zucchini, chopped
- 2 cloves garlic, finely chopped
- 2 1/2 cups tomato puree (passata)
- 1/4 teaspoon dry mustard
- 1/4 teaspoon dried oregano
- 1/4 teaspoon dried basil
- 1 bay leaf
- 2 3/4 tablespoons gluten-free all-purpose baking flour
- 2 tablespoons lactose-free milk
- 3/4 cup lactose-free milk
- 3/4 cup cold vegetable stock
- 2 tablespoons cold vegetable stock
- 2 tablespoons margarine (such as Vitalite®), or to taste
- 1 cup shredded mozzarella-style vegan cheese, divided
- 1 pinch dried parsley, or to taste

- 1 pinch ground black pepper to taste
- 1 (8 ounce) package dry gluten-free lasagna noodles

Direction

- Heat oil in a large saucepan over medium heat. Cook onion and red bell pepper until softened, about 5 minutes. Add zucchini; cook until softened, about 5 minutes more. Stir in garlic until combined. Add tomato puree, mustard, oregano, basil, and bay leaf. Bring to a simmer. Cook vegetable mixture until flavors blend, 10 to 15 minutes.
- Preheat oven to 400 degrees F (200 degrees C). Grease a 9x13-inch baking pan.
- Whisk flour and 2 tablespoons milk together in a bowl until no lumps remain. Mix in 3/4 cup milk and 3/4 cup plus 2 tablespoons vegetable stock. Pour this sauce base into a saucepan over medium-high heat. Add margarine; cook, whisking constantly, until simmering. Reduce heat to low. Add 1/2 cup vegan cheese; stir well. Season with parsley and black pepper. Cook until cheese is fully melted, about 5 minutes.
- Cover the bottom of the baking pan with lasagna noodles. Add a layer of vegetable mixture; top with a thin layer of the cheese sauce. Repeat layering with the remaining noodles, vegetables, and cheese sauce, finishing with a thick blanket of sauce. Sprinkle the remaining 1/2 cup vegan cheese on top.
- Bake in the preheated oven until top is bubbly and browned, about 30 minutes. Let rest before serving until firm, 15 to 20 minutes.

Nutrition Information

- Calories: 235 calories

- Total Fat: 9.2 g
- Cholesterol: < 1 mg
- Sodium: 604 mg
- Total Carbohydrate: 32.8 g
- Protein: 5.8 g

96. Homemade Mac and Cheese

"This is a nice rich mac and cheese. Serve with a salad for a great meatless dinner. Hope you enjoy it."

Serving: 4 | Prep: 20 m | Cook: 30 m | Ready in: 50 m

Ingredients

- 8 ounces uncooked elbow macaroni
- 2 cups shredded sharp Cheddar cheese
- 1/2 cup grated Parmesan cheese
- 3 cups milk
- 1/4 cup butter
- 2 1/2 tablespoons all-purpose flour
- 2 tablespoons butter
- 1/2 cup bread crumbs
- 1 pinch paprika

Direction

- Cook macaroni according to the package directions. Drain.
- In a saucepan, melt butter or margarine over medium heat. Stir in enough flour to make a roux. Add milk to roux slowly, stirring constantly. Stir in cheeses, and cook over low heat until cheese is melted and the sauce is a little thick. Put macaroni in large casserole dish, and pour sauce over macaroni. Stir well.
- Melt butter or margarine in a skillet over medium heat. Add breadcrumbs and brown. Spread over the macaroni and cheese to cover. Sprinkle with a little paprika.
- Bake at 350 degrees F (175 degrees C) for 30 minutes. Serve.

Nutrition Information

- Calories: 858 calories
- Total Fat: 48.7 g
- Cholesterol: 142 mg
- Sodium: 879 mg
- Total Carbohydrate: 66.7 g
- Protein: 37.7 g

97. Homestyle Mushroom Lasagna

"This is a family favorite. It is always requested for birthday dinners. I usually triple this recipe and hope for leftovers. Enjoy!"

Serving: 10 | Prep: 30 m | Cook: 1 h 23 m | Ready in: 1 h 53 m

Ingredients

- 2 tablespoons olive oil
- 4 cups sliced fresh mushrooms
- 2 cups unpeeled shredded zucchini
- 1 onion, chopped
- 1 carrot, shredded
- 3 cups meatless spaghetti sauce
- 1 teaspoon dried oregano
- 1 teaspoon dried basil
- cooking spray
- 12 lasagna noodles
- 2 cups 1% cottage cheese
- 2 cups shredded mozzarella cheese
- 1 (10 ounce) package frozen chopped spinach, thawed and well drained
- 1/4 cup grated Parmesan cheese

Direction

- Heat olive oil in a large saucepan over medium heat. Add mushrooms, zucchini, onion, and carrot; cook and stir until softened, 5 to 10 minutes.
- Stir spaghetti sauce, oregano, and basil into the saucepan; bring to a boil. Reduce heat and simmer sauce, covered, until

- flavors combine, 20 to 30 minutes.
- Preheat oven to 350 degrees F (175 degrees C). Grease a 9x13-inch baking pan with cooking spray.
- Bring a large pot of lightly salted water to a boil. Cook lasagna noodles in the boiling water, stirring occasionally until tender yet firm to the bite, about 8 minutes. Drain.
- Spread a thin layer of sauce in the bottom of the baking pan. Layer 6 lasagna noodles, 1 cup cottage cheese, and 1 cup mozzarella cheese on top of the sauce. Cover mozzarella cheese with spinach. Repeat layers with remaining sauce, lasagna noodles, cottage cheese, and mozzarella cheese. Sprinkle Parmesan cheese on top.
- Bake in the preheated oven until bubbly, 40 to 45 minutes.

Nutrition Information

- Calories: 333 calories
- Total Fat: 12 g
- Cholesterol: 24 mg
- Sodium: 692 mg
- Total Carbohydrate: 38.2 g
- Protein: 19.8 g

98. Hot Tomato Sauce

"I made this up while I was in a cooking class. My whole family likes it. It is medium-hot but you can add more hot chili powder if you like."

Serving: 4 | Prep: 15 m | Cook: 15 m | Ready in: 30 m

Ingredients

- 8 ounces dry pasta
- 1 fresh red chile pepper, chopped
- 1 red bell pepper, chopped
- 1 onion, chopped
- 1 (28 ounce) can diced tomatoes with juice
- 2 tablespoons tomato puree
- 2 teaspoons chili powder

Direction

- Preheat oven to 300 degrees F (150 degrees C). Bring a large pot of lightly salted water to a boil. Add pasta and cook for 8 to 10 minutes or until al dente; drain.
- Meanwhile, in large skillet, sauté chile pepper, bell pepper and onion until soft. Add tomatoes, puree and chili powder and cook 2 minutes more. For a smooth sauce, puree with a hand blender, or puree in batches in food processor.
- Combine pasta and sauce in 9 x 13 baking dish and bake for 15 minutes. Serve hot.

Nutrition Information

- Calories: 283 calories

- Total Fat: 2.9 g
- Cholesterol: 67 mg
- Sodium: 370 mg
- Total Carbohydrate: 52.4 g
- Protein: 10.8 g

99. Italian Veggie Rolls

"These stuffed lasagna noodles really hit the spot. Garnish with chopped parsley or sliced green onions. Serve with a tossed salad, warm garlic bread, and a white zinfandel for a superb meal. You can use fresh, frozen or canned peas for this recipe."

Serving: 5 | Prep: 1 h | Cook: 45 m | Ready in: 1 h 45 m

Ingredients

- 1 cup chopped mushrooms
- 1 onion, chopped
- 1 cup sliced carrots
- 1 cup green peas
- 1 cup chopped broccoli
- 1 clove garlic, minced
- 1/4 cup dry red wine
- 2 cups shredded mozzarella cheese
- 1 egg
- 2 tablespoons olive oil
- 1/4 cup grated Parmesan cheese
- 1 (16 ounce) package lasagna noodles
- 1 (26 ounce) jar spaghetti sauce

Direction

- Cook noodles in a large pot of boiling water until al dente. Rinse, drain, set aside.
- Heat oil in a medium sauté pan. Add mushrooms, onions, carrots, peas, and broccoli; sauté over medium heat until tender. Add wine and garlic; cook five minutes, or until wine has

just about evaporated. Remove from heat, and cool for ten minutes.
- In a medium bowl combine sautéed vegetable mixture, mozzarella cheese, 2 tablespoons Parmesan cheese, and egg. Mix well.
- Pour half of the sauce into the bottom of a 13x9x2inch baking pan. Spread 1/3 cup vegetable mixture over each lasagna noodle then carefully roll up the noodle. Place seam side down in dish. When finished placing all the noodles in the pan, pour remaining pasta sauce evenly over noodles. Cover with aluminum foil.
- Bake at 375 degrees F (190 degrees C) for 35 to 40 minutes. Uncover, and sprinkle remaining Parmesan cheese over noodles. Bake, uncovered, 5 more minutes. Garnish and serve immediately.

Nutrition Information

- Calories: 723 calories
- Total Fat: 23.8 g
- Cholesterol: 79 mg
- Sodium: 1016 mg
- Total Carbohydrate: 97.1 g
- Protein: 30.2 g

100. Jajangmyeon Vegetarian Korean Black Bean Noodles

"Jajangmyeon (jjajangmyeon) is a quick and easy Korean black bean noodle dish that is delicious."

Serving: 2 | Prep: 10 m | Cook: 20 m | Ready in: 30 m

Ingredients

- 1/2 tablespoon canola oil
- 1 clove garlic, minced, or more to taste
- 1/2 cup cubed carrots
- 1/2 cup peeled and cubed potatoes
- salt and ground black pepper to taste
- 1/2 cup peeled and cubed zucchini
- 1/2 cup chopped onion
- 1 tablespoon cornstarch
- 1 tablespoon water
- 1 cup water
- 4 tablespoons black bean paste (chunjang)
- 1 tablespoon white sugar, or to taste
- 1/2 (7 ounce) package jaa jang myun noodles

Direction

- Heat oil in a wok over medium heat. Add garlic, carrot, and potato. Stir and add salt and pepper. Cook until softened, 5 to 7 minutes. Add zucchini and onion; stir.
- Combine cornstarch and water together in a bowl until fully mixed.

- Add water, black bean paste, and sugar to the wok and stir. Add starch mixture to wok slowly while stirring; cook until sauce thickens, 3 to 5 minutes.
- Bring a large pot of lightly salted water to a boil. Cook noodles in boiling water, stirring occasionally, until noodles are tender yet firm to the bite, about 3 minutes. Drain.
- Serve noodles in a large pasta bowl and add black bean mixture on top. Mix well.

Nutrition Information

- Calories: 315 calories
- Total Fat: 5.9 g
- Cholesterol: 0 mg
- Sodium: 401 mg
- Total Carbohydrate: 55.6 g
- Protein: 9.5 g

101. KaesSpaetzle

"A traditional recipe from Bavaria and Baden-Wurtemberg, totally vegetarian, do always serve together with a salad in a sour dressing e.g. simple oil vinegar-dressing!"

Serving: 4 | Prep: 45 m | Cook: 15 m | Ready in: 1 h

Ingredients

- 3 eggs
- 1 3/4 cups all-purpose flour
- 1/2 teaspoon salt
- 1 tablespoon vegetable oil
- 1/2 cup water
- 1/4 cup vegetable oil
- 2 onions, halved and sliced
- 3 cups shredded Swiss cheese
- 1 tablespoon vinegar
- 1 teaspoon chopped fresh parsley, for garnish

Direction

- In a large bowl, combine eggs, flour, salt, 1 tablespoon oil, and 1/2 cup water. Mix until smooth, then let rest for 10 minutes. Meanwhile, heat 1/4 cup oil in a skillet over medium heat. Sauté onion slices until golden brown; set aside. Preheat oven to 300 degrees F (150 degrees C).
- Bring a large pot of lightly salted water to a boil. Place 1/3 of the dough into a spaetzle maker or coarse sieve or collander with holes about 4 millimeters in diameter. Let dough drop into boiling water. Boil until spaetzle rises to the top, then transfer to

a 9 inch casserole dish with a slotted spoon. Cover with 1/3 of the cheese. Repeat layers with remaining spaetzle and cheese. Spoon fried onions over top.
- Bake in preheated oven for 15 minutes, or until cheese is thoroughly melted. Before serving, sprinkle with 1 or 2 tablespoons vinegar, and sprinkle with chopped parsley.

Nutrition Information

- Calories: 733 calories
- Total Fat: 43.9 g
- Cholesterol: 214 mg
- Sodium: 502 mg
- Total Carbohydrate: 51.5 g
- Protein: 32.8 g

102. Kicked Up Mac and Cheese

"This ain't your grandma's mac and cheese."

Serving: 8 | Prep: 30 m | Cook: 40 m | Ready in: 1 h 10 m

Ingredients

- 1 1/2 cups rotelle pasta
- 4 tablespoons butter, divided
- 1/4 cup all-purpose flour
- 3 cups whole milk
- 1 teaspoon dry mustard
- 3/4 teaspoon salt
- 1/2 teaspoon ground white pepper
- 3 teaspoons hot pepper sauce
- 1 cup shredded pepperjack cheese
- 1 1/2 cups shredded sharp Cheddar cheese
- 1/2 cup grated Parmesan cheese
- 1/3 cup dry bread crumbs
- 2 teaspoons chili powder

Direction

- Preheat oven to 375 degrees F (190 degrees C).
- Bring a large pot of lightly salted water to a boil. Add pasta and cook for 8 to 10 minutes or until al dente; drain.
- In a large saucepan over medium heat, melt 2 tablespoons butter. Whisk in flour and cook, stirring, 1 minute. A little at a time, whisk in milk, mustard, salt, pepper and hot sauce. Bring to a gentle boil, stirring constantly. Boil 1 minute, then remove from heat and whisk in pepperjack, Cheddar and Parmesan

until smooth. Stir in cooked pasta and pour into shallow 2 quart baking dish.
- Melt remaining 2 tablespoons butter. Stir in bread crumbs and chili powder. Sprinkle over macaroni mixture.
- Bake in preheated oven 30 minutes. Let stand 10 minutes before serving.

Nutrition Information

- Calories: 352 calories
- Total Fat: 23.3 g
- Cholesterol: 69 mg
- Sodium: 690 mg
- Total Carbohydrate: 19.6 g
- Protein: 16.4 g

103. Lasagna Roll Ups

"This is a good freeze and eat later meal. It uses tofu, but you'd never know it! My cooking co-op loved this recipe! You can individually freeze the roll ups on a cookie sheet and place in a freezer bag."

Serving: 12 | Prep: 30 m | Cook: 30 m | Ready in: 1 h

Ingredients

- 1 (16 ounce) package uncooked lasagna noodles
- 1 pound mozzarella cheese, shredded
- 1 (15 ounce) container ricotta cheese
- 1 pound firm tofu
- 1 (10 ounce) package frozen chopped spinach - thawed, drained and squeezed dry
- 2 cups grated Parmesan cheese
- 1 (28 ounce) jar pasta sauce

Direction

- Bring a large pot of lightly salted water to a boil. Cook lasagna noodles for 5 to 8 minutes, or until just slightly underdone; drain and rinse.
- In a large mixing bowl, mix together grated cheese, ricotta cheese, tofu, frozen spinach, and 1 cup Parmesan cheese.
- Lay out a noodle. Spread a layer of the cheese mixture on the noodle, then add a thin layer of sauce. Roll the noodle up, and place seam side down in a 13x9 pan. Repeat for other noodles. Top with remaining sauce and Parmesan cheese.
- Bake in a preheated 350 degree F (175 degree C) oven for 30 min, or until hot and bubbly.

Nutrition Information

- Calories: 455 calories
- Total Fat: 18.7 g
- Cholesterol: 48 mg
- Sodium: 775 mg
- Total Carbohydrate: 42.2 g
- Protein: 31.3 g

104. Lasagna Spinach RollUps

"For variety, substitute one pound of cooked Italian sausage for one box of the spinach. You can use your own favorite home cooked tomato sauce or use sauce from a jar in place of the sauce in this recipe."

Serving: 8 | Prep: 25 m | Cook: 40 m | Ready in: 1 h 5 m

Ingredients

- 1 (16 ounce) package lasagna noodles
- 2 tablespoons butter
- 2/3 cup chopped red bell pepper
- 2/3 cup chopped fresh mushrooms
- 1/2 cup chopped onion
- 2 cups small curd cottage cheese
- 2 (10 ounce) packages frozen chopped spinach
- 2 eggs, lightly beaten
- 6 tablespoons grated Parmesan cheese, divided
- 1 teaspoon black pepper
- 2 (15 ounce) cans tomato sauce
- 2 teaspoons dried marjoram
- 1 teaspoon white sugar
- 1/2 teaspoon garlic powder
- 2/3 cup shredded mozzarella cheese

Direction

- Preheat oven to 350 degrees F (175 degrees C).
- Bring a large pot of water to a boil. Add lasagna pasta and cook for 8 to 10 minutes or until al dente; drain and pat dry.

- In a large skillet sauté in butter the red bell pepper, mushrooms and onion until tender. In a bowl combine the sautéed vegetable mixture, cottage cheese, spinach, eggs, 4 tablespoons of the Parmesan cheese and pepper; mix well.
- In a large skillet, heat tomato sauce, marjoram, sugar and garlic powder for 5 minutes.
- Spread 1/3 cup filling on each noodle. Roll up and place in greased 9x13 baking dish. Pour tomato sauce mixture over lasagna rolls. Sprinkle with mozzarella cheese and remaining Parmesan cheese. Cover and bake in a preheated oven for 40 minutes.

Nutrition Information

- Calories: 399 calories
- Total Fat: 11.2 g
- Cholesterol: 72 mg
- Sodium: 988 mg
- Total Carbohydrate: 54 g
- Protein: 24.2 g

105. Lasagna Spirals

"This is a good meatless dish that is very easy to make and so good too. I make several at one time and freeze what I don't use for dinner. Then I just take from freezer what I need, thaw, bake, and voila! You could be creative with these too and add other veggies."

Serving: 10 | Prep: 30 m | Cook: 30 m | Ready in: 1 h

Ingredients

- 10 wide lasagna noodles
- 2 (10 ounce) packages chopped frozen broccoli, thawed and drained
- 1 (15 ounce) container ricotta cheese
- 2 cups shredded mozzarella cheese
- 4 green onions, chopped
- 2 teaspoons dried basil
- 1/4 teaspoon ground nutmeg
- 1 (32 ounce) jar spaghetti sauce
- 1/2 cup grated Parmesan cheese

Direction

- Preheat oven to 350 degrees F (175 degrees C). Lightly grease a 9x13 inch baking dish.
- Bring a large pot of lightly salted water to a boil. Add noodles and cook for 8 to 10 minutes or until al dente; drain and rinse.
- In a large bowl combine broccoli, ricotta cheese, mozzarella cheese, green onions, basil and nutmeg.
- Spread about 1/2 cup of the broccoli mixture along each noodle. Roll noodles to form spirals. Place in prepared dish.

Spoon spaghetti sauce on and around spirals, and top with Parmesan cheese.
- Bake in preheated oven for 30 minutes.

Nutrition Information

- Calories: 315 calories
- Total Fat: 11.3 g
- Cholesterol: 33 mg
- Sodium: 638 mg
- Total Carbohydrate: 36.1 g
- Protein: 18.4 g

106. Lazy Pierogi

"For this tasty pierogi casserole, sauerkraut, onion, mushrooms, and pasta are combined and baked in a rich, buttery sauce. If you are making this ahead and are going to reheat it in the oven you may have to add a little water. If cold, bake at 350 degrees for 1 1/2 to 2 hours."

Serving: 8 | Prep: 10 m | Cook: 1 h 20 m | Ready in: 1 h 30 m

Ingredients

- 3 pounds sauerkraut
- 1 onion, chopped
- 1 pound uncooked rotini pasta
- 1 pound fresh mushrooms, chopped
- 1/2 pound butter
- 2 (10.75 ounce) cans condensed cream of mushroom soup

Direction

- Place the sauerkraut and onion in a large skillet over medium-low heat with enough water to cover. Simmer 1 hour, or until most of the water has cooked off.
- Bring a large pot of lightly salted water to a boil. Add rotini and cook for 8 to 10 minutes or until al dente; drain.
- In a medium skillet over medium heat, sauté the mushrooms in 2 tablespoons of the butter for about 5 minutes.
- Stir the remaining butter, cooked pasta, and cream of mushroom soup into the sauerkraut mixture. Cook and stir 15 minutes, or until heated through.

Nutrition Information

- Calories: 529 calories
- Total Fat: 28.8 g
- Cholesterol: 61 mg
- Sodium: 1787 mg
- Total Carbohydrate: 57.9 g
- Protein: 12.3 g

107. Lemon Coconut ThaiInspired Pasta

"This is a strange combination of ingredients that creates a very refreshing, flavorful one-plate meal! It is super fast and easy to prepare. It is also extremely versatile - use what you have and like. This dish can be adapted to be vegetarian or vegan-friendly."

Serving: 4 | Prep: 25 m | Cook: 20 m | Ready in: 45 m

Ingredients

- 1/2 (8 ounce) package spaghetti
- 1 cup coconut milk
- 1/2 cup dry white wine
- 1/4 cup fresh lemon juice
- 2 tablespoons olive oil
- 3 cloves garlic, minced, or more to taste
- 1 teaspoon white sugar (optional)
- 1/4 teaspoon salt
- 1/8 teaspoon red pepper flakes
- 1/8 teaspoon ground black pepper
- 1 1/2 cups cooked shredded chicken
- 2 roma (plum) tomatoes, diced
- 1/2 cup bean sprouts
- 1/4 cup chopped fresh basil
- 1/4 cup chopped fresh parsley
- 3 green onions, chopped
- 1 (5 ounce) package arugula
- 1 lemon, zested

Direction

- Bring a large pot of lightly salted water to a boil. Cook spaghetti in the boiling water, stirring occasionally until cooked through but firm to the bite, about 12 minutes. Drain and return spaghetti to pot.
- Whisk coconut milk, white wine, lemon juice, olive oil, garlic, sugar, salt, red pepper flakes, and black pepper in a small saucepan over medium heat; simmer until flavors combine, 5 to 6 minutes.
- Stir chicken, tomatoes, bean sprouts, basil, parsley, and green onions into pasta; cook over low heat until warmed through, 3 to 5 minutes. Add coconut sauce; stir to combine. Serve pasta over a bed of arugula. Sprinkle with lemon zest.

Nutrition Information

- Calories: 400 calories
- Total Fat: 22.2 g
- Cholesterol: 26 mg
- Sodium: 194 mg
- Total Carbohydrate: 30.8 g
- Protein: 16.5 g

108. Lemon Parmesan Spaghetti

"This is one of those 'much more than the sum of its parts' recipes. It's great with a salad, perfect for vegetarians and children, and makes a wonderful side dish with chicken or seafood."

Serving: 4 | Prep: 15 m | Cook: 30 m | Ready in: 45 m

Ingredients

- 8 ounces spaghetti
- 1/3 cup unsalted butter
- 1 (8 ounce) container sour cream
- 1 teaspoon lemon zest
- 3 tablespoons fresh lemon juice
- 3 tablespoons chopped fresh parsley
- 1/4 cup grated Parmesan cheese
- salt and ground black pepper to taste

Direction

- Preheat oven to 400 degrees F (200 degrees C).
- Cook spaghetti according to package directions until al dente. Drain and place spaghetti in a greased 1.5 quart casserole dish.
- Melt butter in medium saucepan over low heat. Remove from heat, and stir in sour cream, lemon peel, and lemon juice. Mix until smooth. Pour mixture over spaghetti in casserole dish. Mix well
- Bake 15 to 20 minutes in the preheated oven, or until heated through. Remove from oven, and add grated Parmesan cheese

and parsley. Season with salt and freshly ground pepper to taste. Serve immediately.

Nutrition Information

- Calories: 491 calories
- Total Fat: 29.5 g
- Cholesterol: 70 mg
- Sodium: 114 mg
- Total Carbohydrate: 45.7 g
- Protein: 11.3 g

109. Linguine with Portobello Mushrooms

"Portobello mushrooms are a really good meat substitute, especially when they are grilled. If possible, use fresh herbs in this recipe."

Serving: 8 | Prep: 15 m | Cook: 30 m | Ready in: 45 m

Ingredients

- 4 portobello mushroom caps
- 2 tablespoons extra virgin olive oil
- 1 pound linguine pasta
- 1 teaspoon red wine vinegar
- 1 teaspoon chopped fresh oregano
- 1 teaspoon chopped fresh basil
- 1/2 teaspoon chopped fresh rosemary
- 2 cloves garlic, peeled and crushed
- 2 teaspoons lemon juice
- salt and pepper to taste

Direction

- Preheat the oven broiler.
- Bring a large pot of lightly salted water to a boil. Add linguine, and cook for 9 to 13 minutes or until al dente; drain.
- Brush the mushrooms with 1/2 the olive oil, and arrange on a medium baking sheet. Broil in the prepared oven 6 to 8 minutes, turning frequently, until browned and tender.
- Cut the mushrooms into 1/4 inch slices, and place in a medium bowl. Mix with the remaining olive oil, red wine vinegar,

oregano, basil, rosemary, garlic, and lemon juice. Season with salt and pepper.
- In a large bowl, toss together cooked linguine and the mushroom mixture.

Nutrition Information

- Calories: 250 calories
- Total Fat: 4.8 g
- Cholesterol: 0 mg
- Sodium: 152 mg
- Total Carbohydrate: 44.6 g
- Protein: 9 g

110. Linguini with Vegetables

"An easy, colorful, dish that takes just 30 minutes. For variety, you can add two cups of chopped, cooked chicken or shrimp."

Serving: 3

Ingredients

- 1 pound linguini pasta
- 3 tablespoons olive oil
- 1 small zucchini, thinly sliced
- 1 yellow squash, thinly sliced
- 2 carrots, sliced thin
- 1 red bell pepper, thinly sliced
- 1/2 onion, sliced
- 1 tablespoon salt-free herb and spice blend
- 4 cloves crushed garlic
- 1/4 cup white wine
- 1 tablespoon lemon juice

Direction

- In a large pot with boiling salted water cook linguini pasta until al dente. Drain well.
- Meanwhile, in a large skillet heat olive oil and add thinly sliced zucchini, squash, carrots, red bell pepper, onions, salt-free spice blend, and minced garlic. Cook on medium-high for five minutes, stirring frequently. Add white wine and lemon juice and continue cooking until vegetables are crisp-tender and liquid has reduced, about 5 to 10 minutes.

- Toss cooked and drained pasta with sautéed vegetables and serve.

Nutrition Information

- Calories: 739 calories
- Total Fat: 17.4 g
- Cholesterol: 0 mg
- Sodium: 46 mg
- Total Carbohydrate: 124 g
- Protein: 22.7 g

111. Lo Mein Noodles

"This was a blend of multiple lo mein recipes I found. Add your favorite meat for a main dish, or make as a side dish to your favorite homemade chinese dinner. If you use meat, cook the meat in the pan first, and then pull out and set aside."

Serving: 4 | Prep: 15 m | Cook: 25 m | Ready in: 40 m

Ingredients

- 1 (8 ounce) package spaghetti
- 3 tablespoons low-sodium soy sauce
- 2 tablespoons teriyaki sauce
- 2 tablespoons honey
- 1/4 teaspoon ground ginger
- 2 tablespoons vegetable oil
- 3 stalks celery, sliced
- 2 large carrots, cut into large matchsticks
- 1/2 sweet onion, thinly sliced
- 2 green onions, sliced

Direction

- Bring a large pot of lightly salted water to a boil. Cook spaghetti in the boiling water, stirring occasionally until cooked through but firm to the bite, about 12 minutes; drain. Rinse spaghetti with cold water to cool; drain.
- Whisk soy sauce, teriyaki sauce, honey, and ground ginger together in a bowl.
- Heat oil in a large skillet or wok over high heat. Cook and stir celery, carrots, sweet onion, and green onion in the hot oil until slightly tender, 5 to 7 minutes; add spaghetti and sauce

mixture. Continue to cook, tossing to mix, until the noodles and sauce are hot, about 5 minutes more.

Nutrition Information

- Calories: 344 calories
- Total Fat: 7.8 g
- Cholesterol: 0 mg
- Sodium: 798 mg
- Total Carbohydrate: 59.6 g
- Protein: 9.4 g

112. Lovely Linguine

"This linguine is served with a buttery thyme and roasted red pepper sauce. It is delicious."

Serving: 8 | Prep: 15 m | Cook: 15 m | Ready in: 30 m

Ingredients

- 1 (16 ounce) package uncooked linguine pasta
- 2 tablespoons olive oil
- 3/4 cup butter
- 3 cloves garlic, chopped
- 2 tablespoons fresh thyme leaves
- 5 roasted red peppers, drained and coarsely chopped

Direction

- Bring a large pot of lightly salted water to a boil. Add linguine and olive oil, cook for 8 to 10 minutes, until al dente, and drain.
- Melt 2 tablespoons butter in a saucepan over medium heat. Stir in garlic, and cook until golden brown. Mix in remaining butter, thyme, and roasted red peppers. Continue to cook and stir until heated through. Serve over the cooked pasta.

Nutrition Information

- Calories: 405 calories
- Total Fat: 22 g
- Cholesterol: 46 mg
- Sodium: 379 mg
- Total Carbohydrate: 43.9 g

- Protein: 7.9 g

113. Low Fat Cheesy Spinach and Eggplant Lasagna

"Lasagna recipe with vegetables and cheese!"

Serving: 12 | Prep: 40 m | Cook: 45 m | Ready in: 1 h 25 m

Ingredients

- 12 whole wheat lasagna noodles, dry
- 1 teaspoon olive oil
- 2 tablespoons olive oil
- 3 cloves garlic, minced
- 1 eggplant, cubed
- 1 (28 ounce) can Italian herb-flavored tomato sauce
- 1 cup part-skim ricotta cheese
- 1 cup low-fat cottage cheese
- 1 cup shredded part-skim mozzarella cheese
- 1/4 cup shredded Parmesan cheese
- 1/2 teaspoon salt
- 1/2 teaspoon ground black pepper
- 1 egg
- 2 1/2 cups frozen chopped spinach, thawed and squeezed dry

Direction

- Preheat oven to 375 degrees F (190 degrees C).
- Bring a large pot of water to a boil.
- Drop lasagna noodles into water and add 1 teaspoon of olive oil. Cook until noodles are tender but still slightly firm, about 8 minutes.

- Drain water from the noodles and let cool.
- Heat 2 tablespoons olive oil in a large skillet over medium heat.
- Cook and stir garlic and eggplant chunks until eggplant is partially cooked, about 7 minutes.
- Pour tomato sauce into the skillet and simmer until eggplant is tender, 10 to 15 minutes.
- Combine ricotta cheese, cottage cheese, mozzarella cheese, Parmesan cheese, salt, black pepper, and egg in a bowl.
- Mix spinach into ricotta cheese mixture.
- Spread a layer of tomato sauce mixture into the bottom of a 9x12-inch baking dish.
- Place 4 noodles on top of the sauce, overlapping if necessary.
- Spoon 1/3 of the remaining tomato sauce over noodles.
- Spread 1/3 of the ricotta mixture over the tomato sauce
- Repeat layers twice more, starting with noodles and following with sauce and ricotta mixture.
- Top the lasagna with mozzarella cheese.
- Bake in preheated oven until the ricotta filling is set and mozzarella cheese topping is lightly browned, 45 minutes to 1 hour.

Nutrition Information

- Calories: 206 calories
- Total Fat: 7.6 g
- Cholesterol: 31 mg
- Sodium: 660 mg
- Total Carbohydrate: 23.2 g
- Protein: 13.7 g

114. LowCalorie Vegetarian Filipino Pancit

"Growing up with a Filipino mother, I had the pleasure of eating a lot of great Filipino recipes that, at the time, I took for granted. Pancit was just a side dish at special meals. My mother loves it. It always appeared on special occasions like Christmas or Thanksgiving, but never for dinner on any other day. Now I crave Filipino food daily. So when I have the chance to incorporate it into any old dinner, I will. Garnish with sesame seeds, scallions, or nuts."

Serving: 4 | Prep: 15 m | Cook: 47 m | Ready in: 1 h 17 m

Ingredients

- 2 tablespoons extra-virgin olive oil, divided, or to taste
- 1 spaghetti squash, halved and seeded
- 2 carrots, chopped, or to taste
- 2 stalks celery, chopped, or to taste
- 1 cup shredded cabbage, or to taste
- 1 cup frozen shelled edamame (green soybeans)
- 1 zucchini, chopped, or to taste
- 2 tablespoons soy sauce, or to taste
- ground black pepper to taste

Direction

- Preheat the oven to 400 degrees F (200 degrees C). Lightly coat a baking pan with 1 tablespoon olive oil.
- Place spaghetti squash, cut-side down, on the prepared baking pan.
- Bake in the preheated oven until tender, about 40 minutes. Let cool until safe to handle, about 15 minutes.

- Separate strands of spaghetti squash with a fork and scoop into a large bowl.
- Heat 1 tablespoon olive oil in a large skillet over medium-high heat. Add carrots, celery, cabbage, edamame, and zucchini. Sauté, adding soy sauce and pepper, until tender but still crunchy, about 7 minutes.
- Transfer cooked vegetables to the bowl with the spaghetti squash and toss. Taste and season as desired.

Nutrition Information

- Calories: 233 calories
- Total Fat: 12.3 g
- Cholesterol: 0 mg
- Sodium: 523 mg
- Total Carbohydrate: 24.2 g
- Protein: 10.8 g

115. Lucys Mac and Corn

"This recipe came from my high school cafeteria's cook, Lucy. It's my favorite school lunch dish! (Casey's mom has found that 1/2 stick of margarine and reduced-fat Velveeta results in an equal taste with less fat.)"

Serving: 7

Ingredients

- 1 (14.75 ounce) can creamed corn
- 1 (11.25 ounce) can corn
- 1 cup macaroni
- 1/2 cup butter
- 8 ounces cubed processed cheese food

Direction

- Mix together creamed corn, whole kernel corn, and uncooked macaroni. Slice the butter or margarine, and mix into the corn mixture along with the cheese. Place in a buttered casserole dish. Cover.
- Bake at 350 degrees F (175 degrees C) for 30 minutes. Uncover, stir, and bake uncovered for 30 more minutes.

Nutrition Information

- Calories: 350 calories
- Total Fat: 21.8 g
- Cholesterol: 56 mg
- Sodium: 671 mg
- Total Carbohydrate: 31.5 g

- Protein: 10.4 g

116. Mac and Cheese II

"This recipe is so simple to make! It can be a side dish with meatloaf and stewed tomatoes or hold it's own. Enough to make 4 side dishes or 2 main dishes."

Serving: 4 | Prep: 20 m | Cook: 45 m | Ready in: 1 h 5 m

Ingredients

- 8 ounces elbow macaroni
- 2 tablespoons butter
- 1/4 cup all-purpose flour
- 2 cups milk
- 1 cup shredded Cheddar cheese
- 8 ounces cubed processed cheese food

Direction

- In a large pot with boiling salted water cook elbow macaroni until al dente. Drain.
- In a medium saucepan, over medium heat melt butter or margarine. Whisk flour and stir vigorously. Add milk and cook until thick and bubbly, about 5 to 7 minutes. Add cheeses and stir until completely melted.
- In a large bowl mix together the drained pasta and cheese sauce mixture. Toss to coat evenly.
- Pour into a greased 2 quart casserole dish. Bake in a preheated 350 degree F (175 degrees C) oven for 30 minutes. Let stand 10 minutes before serving.

Nutrition Information

- Calories: 650 calories
- Total Fat: 32.3 g
- Cholesterol: 91 mg
- Sodium: 818 mg
- Total Carbohydrate: 58.6 g
- Protein: 30.4 g

117. Mac and Shews Vegan Mac and Cheese

"Cashews are basically vegan dairy. Blend them with a little liquid and you've got a smooth cream, similar to half-and-half. Mixed with broth, nutritional yeast, miso and seasonings along with the macaroni and you've got delish mac 'n cheese."

Serving: 4 | Prep: 5 m | Cook: 15 m | Ready in: 20 m

Ingredients

- 1 cup unroasted cashews
- 1 cup vegetable broth
- 3 tablespoons nutritional yeast flakes
- 3 tablespoons fresh lemon juice
- 2 teaspoons white miso
- 2 teaspoons onion powder
- 1/2 teaspoon salt, or to taste
- black pepper to taste
- 8 ounces small shell pasta or macaroni
- 1 1/2 cups arugula (optional)

Direction

- Blend cashews, broth, yeast, lemon juice, miso, and onion powder in a high-powered blender (such as a Vitamix(R)), scraping down sides with a spatula until completely smooth. Season with salt and pepper, keeping in mind that you want it just a little saltier than usual because it's going to be poured over other ingredients.
- Meanwhile, bring a pot of salted water to a boil and cook pasta according to package directions.

- Drain, return to pot, and stir in cashew sauce. Cook over low heat, stirring, until sauce thickens a bit and everything is deliciously creamy, about 3 minutes. Stir in arugula (if using) and add more salt, if needed. Serve immediately.

Nutrition Information

- Calories: 430 calories
- Total Fat: 16.8 g
- Cholesterol: 0 mg
- Sodium: 525 mg
- Total Carbohydrate: 57.2 g
- Protein: 17.6 g

118. Macaroni and Cheese III

"A rich macaroni and cheese recipe, with lots of sharp Cheddar cheese. Especially good with the addition of browned ground beef or spicy sausage."

Serving: 6 | Prep: 15 m | Cook: 10 m | Ready in: 35 m

Ingredients

- 1 (16 ounce) package macaroni
- 2 1/2 cups shredded sharp Cheddar cheese
- 1/2 cup plain yogurt
- 1 tablespoon butter
- 1 (14.5 ounce) can stewed tomatoes
- 1/8 teaspoon celery seed
- salt to taste
- ground black pepper to taste
- 1/4 tablespoon dried basil

Direction

- In a large pot cook macaroni pasta in boiling salted water until al dente. Drain well.
- In a large saucepan over medium heat, melt the grated Cheddar cheese, plain yogurt, butter or margarine, and tomatoes. Cook until smooth. Add salt, black pepper, basil to taste, celery seed and cooked pasta to saucepan. Stir until blended.
- Turn off the heat and let sit for 10 minutes with lid on, stirring occasionally. Serve hot.

Nutrition Information

- Calories: 557 calories
- Total Fat: 22.6 g
- Cholesterol: 67 mg
- Sodium: 539 mg
- Total Carbohydrate: 62.4 g
- Protein: 25.8 g

119. Macaroni and Cheese V

"This is my mom's recipe for macaroni and cheese with a bread crumb topping and a little dry mustard for zip. It is great!! You can make it more or less cheesy, depends on your taste."

Serving: 6 | Prep: 15 m | Cook: 35 m | Ready in: 50 m

Ingredients

- 3/4 cup dry bread crumbs
- 2 tablespoons melted butter
- 8 ounces macaroni
- 2 tablespoons butter
- 1 small onion, minced
- 1 tablespoon all-purpose flour
- salt and pepper to taste
- 1/4 teaspoon dry mustard
- 1 1/2 cups milk
- 2 cups shredded Cheddar cheese

Direction

- Preheat oven to 350 degrees F (175 degrees C). Grease a 2 quart casserole dish. Place the bread crumbs into a small bowl and mix well with the melted butter; set aside.
- Bring a large pot of lightly salted water to a boil. Add macaroni and cook for 8 to 10 minutes or until al dente; drain, then place into prepared casserole dish.
- While the pasta is cooking, melt 2 tablespoons butter in a saucepan over medium heat. Stir in the minced onion and cook until the onion softens and turns translucent, about 5 minutes.

- Stir in the flour, pepper, salt, and dry mustard until incorporated, then pour in the milk and bring to a simmer. Simmer, stirring constantly until the milk has thickened, about 10 minutes. Take the milk off of the heat and stir in the Cheddar cheese until melted. Pour cheese sauce over the macaroni, then sprinkle evenly with buttered bread crumbs.
- Bake until the top is golden and bubbly, about 20 minutes.

Nutrition Information

- Calories: 461 calories
- Total Fat: 23 g
- Cholesterol: 65 mg
- Sodium: 414 mg
- Total Carbohydrate: 43.9 g
- Protein: 19 g

120. Manicotti

"Delicious! Serve with a crispy salad and garlic bread, and you'll have a dish your family will love! The kids like to help stuff the noodles too!"

Serving: 4 | Prep: 30 m | Cook: 45 m | Ready in: 1 h 15 m

Ingredients

- 1 pint part-skim ricotta cheese
- 8 ounces shredded mozzarella cheese
- 3/4 cup grated Parmesan cheese
- 2 eggs
- 1 teaspoon dried parsley
- salt to taste
- ground black pepper to taste
- 1 (16 ounce) jar spaghetti sauce
- 5 1/2 ounces manicotti pasta

Direction

- Cook manicotti in boiling water until done. Drain, and rinse with cold water.
- Preheat oven to 350 degrees F (175 degrees C).
- In a large bowl, combine ricotta, mozzarella, and 1/2 cup Parmesan, eggs, parsley, and salt and pepper. Mix well.
- Pour 1/2 cup sauce into an 11x17 inch baking dish. Fill each manicotti shell with 3 tablespoons cheese mixture, and arrange over sauce. Pour remaining sauce over top, and sprinkle with remaining Parmesan cheese.
- Bake 45 minutes, or until bubbly.

Nutrition Information

- Calories: 676 calories
- Total Fat: 30.9 g
- Cholesterol: 189 mg
- Sodium: 1255 mg
- Total Carbohydrate: 53.2 g
- Protein: 46 g

121. Manicotti Pancakes I

"Make these shells from scratch, stuff with seasoned cheese or ground meat, and bake with tomato sauce and cheese in a moderate oven for 35 minutes."

Serving: 6 | Prep: 5 m | Cook: 10 m | Ready in: 15 m

Ingredients

- 1 cup all-purpose flour
- 4 eggs
- 1 tablespoon olive oil
- 1 teaspoon salt
- 1 cup water

Direction

- Combine flour, eggs, olive oil, salt and water in a medium bowl; stir until smooth. Heat a 7 inch skillet over medium-high heat and lightly brush with olive oil. Ladle enough batter into pan to cover the bottom. Cook until top is set and bottom is brown, about 30 seconds. Lift pancake onto parchment paper and repeat. Stuff with meat or cheese filling, top with tomato sauce and bake.

Nutrition Information

- Calories: 161 calories
- Total Fat: 7.6 g
- Cholesterol: 134 mg
- Sodium: 457 mg
- Total Carbohydrate: 16.2 g

- Protein: 6.7 g

122. Manicotti Pancakes II

"This recipe came from a very old Italian family and it is super!"

Serving: 12 | Prep: 5 m | Cook: 10 m | Ready in: 15 m

Ingredients

- 3 eggs
- 1 cup milk
- 1 cup all-purpose flour

Direction

- Beat eggs and milk together in large bowl. Beat in flour until batter is smooth. Lightly coat an 8 inch skillet or crepe pan on medium-high heat with cooking spray. Make one pancake at a time by dropping a large spoonful of batter onto pan and tilting to cover the whole surface of the pan evenly. Cook until golden, turning once, about 2 minutes per pancake.

Nutrition Information

- Calories: 66 calories
- Total Fat: 1.7 g
- Cholesterol: 48 mg
- Sodium: 26 mg
- Total Carbohydrate: 9 g
- Protein: 3.3 g

123. MeatFree Stuffed Shells

"Veg-friendly stuffed shells."

Serving: 6 | Prep: 15 m | Cook: 55 m | Ready in: 1 h 10 m

Ingredients

- 1 (12 ounce) box jumbo pasta shells
- 2 tablespoons butter
- 1 cup sliced mushrooms
- 1/2 onion, chopped
- 2 cloves garlic, minced
- 1 (12 ounce) package firm tofu
- 1/2 cup dry bread crumbs
- 1/2 (10 ounce) package frozen chopped spinach, thawed and drained
- 1/4 cup grated Parmesan cheese
- 1 teaspoon Italian seasoning
- 1 egg (optional)
- 2 cups shredded mozzarella cheese
- 1 (16 ounce) jar spaghetti sauce, or as needed

Direction

- Preheat oven to 350 degrees F (175 degrees C).
- Fill a large pot with lightly salted water and bring to a rolling boil over high heat. Once the water is boiling, stir in the shell pasta, and return to a boil. Cook the pasta uncovered, stirring occasionally, until the pasta has cooked through, but is still firm to the bite, about 13 minutes. Drain well in a colander set in the sink, and set aside.

- Melt the butter in a skillet, and cook and stir the mushrooms, onion, and garlic until the onion is translucent, about 7 minutes. Mash the tofu roughly with a fork in a bowl, and mix in the mushroom mixture, bread crumbs, spinach, Parmesan cheese, and Italian seasoning; stir until combined. If mixture seems crumbly, stir in an egg.
- Pour enough pasta sauce into the bottom of a 9x13-inch baking dish to coat the bottom. Fill each shell with about 1 1/2 tablespoon of filling, and place into the dish in a single layer. Spoon remaining sauce on top of shells. If there's any remaining filling, scatter that over the sauce, and sprinkle the mozzarella cheese over the top. Cover the dish with aluminum foil.
- Bake in the preheated oven until the filling is hot and set and the cheese is melted and bubbling, about 30 minutes.

Nutrition Information

- Calories: 526 calories
- Total Fat: 17.8 g
- Cholesterol: 70 mg
- Sodium: 721 mg
- Total Carbohydrate: 64.5 g
- Protein: 27.4 g

124. Meatless Eggplant Lasagna

"Meatless Monday done right!"

Serving: 9 | Prep: 30 m | Cook: 45 m | Ready in: 1 h 25 m

Ingredients

- cooking spray
- Eggplant:
- 2 large eggs, lightly beaten
- 1 tablespoon water
- 2 cups panko bread crumbs
- 1/4 cup grated Parmigiano-Reggiano cheese
- 2 eggplants, peeled and sliced into 1/2-inch rounds
- Filling:
- 1 (16 ounce) container ricotta cheese
- 1/2 cup chopped fresh basil
- 1 large egg, lightly beaten
- 1/4 cup grated Parmigiano-Reggiano cheese
- 1 1/2 teaspoons minced garlic
- 1/2 teaspoon crushed red pepper
- 1/4 teaspoon salt
- 1 (24 ounce) jar marinara sauce
- 1 yellow bell pepper, diced
- 1 green bell pepper, diced
- 1/4 teaspoon salt
- 8 ounces thinly sliced mozzarella cheese
- 3/4 cup finely grated Fontina cheese

Direction

- Preheat the oven to 375 degrees F (190 degrees C). Coat 2 baking sheets and a 9x13-inch baking dish with cooking spray.
- Stir together 2 eggs and water in a shallow dish. Combine panko and Parmigiano-Reggiano cheese in a second shallow dish. Dip eggplant slices in egg mixture and dredge in panko mixture, pressing gently to adhere and shaking off excess. Place on prepared baking sheets.
- Bake in the preheated oven until golden, turning once and rotating baking sheets after 15 minutes, about 30 minutes total.
- Combine ricotta cheese, basil, 1 egg, Parmigiano-Reggiano, garlic, red pepper, and salt in a bowl to make filling.
- Spoon 1/2 cup marinara sauce into the prepared baking dish. Layer 1/2 the eggplant slices over sauce and sprinkle with 1/8 teaspoon salt. Top with 3/4 cup marinara sauce. Spread 1/2 the ricotta mixture on top; add 1/2 the yellow and green bell peppers and top with 1/3 the mozzarella cheese and 1/4 the Fontina cheese. Repeat layers, ending with 1 cup marinara sauce. Cover tightly with aluminum foil coated with cooking spray.
- Bake in the preheated oven for 35 minutes.
- Remove aluminum foil; top with remaining mozzarella cheese and Fontina cheese. Continue baking until sauce is bubbly and cheese melts, about 10 minutes more. Cool 10 minutes before serving.

Nutrition Information

- Calories: 385 calories
- Total Fat: 17.5 g
- Cholesterol: 112 mg
- Sodium: 954 mg
- Total Carbohydrate: 39.9 g
- Protein: 24 g

125. Mediterranean Pasta with Greens

"A delicious blend of greens, olives, garlic, and sun-dried tomatoes tossed with pasta. Delicious and satisfying."

Serving: 8 | Prep: 15 m | Cook: 20 m | Ready in: 35 m

Ingredients

- 1 (16 ounce) package dry fusilli pasta
- 1 bunch Swiss chard, stems removed
- 2 tablespoons olive oil
- 1/2 cup oil-packed sun-dried tomatoes, chopped
- 1/2 cup pitted, chopped kalamata olives
- 1/2 cup pitted, chopped green olives
- 1 clove garlic, minced
- 1/4 cup fresh grated Parmesan cheese

Direction

- Bring a large pot of lightly salted water to a boil. Stir in pasta, cook for 10 to 12 minutes, until al dente, and drain.
- Place chard in a microwave safe bowl. Fill bowl about 1/2 full with water. Cook on High in the microwave 5 minutes, until limp; drain.
- Heat the oil in a skillet over medium heat. Stir in the sun-dried tomatoes, kalamata olives, green olives, and garlic. Mix in the chard. Cook and stir until tender. Toss with pasta and sprinkle with Parmesan cheese to serve.

Nutrition Information

- Calories: 296 calories
- Total Fat: 9.7 g
- Cholesterol: 2 mg
- Sodium: 467 mg
- Total Carbohydrate: 44.6 g
- Protein: 9.6 g

126. Mediterranean Whole Wheat Pasta Toss

"This delicious blend of many robust ingredients will explode with flavor in your mouth. This was one of those nights where we sort of just opened the fridge to see what we had and this is what we ended up with. You can adjust any ingredients to suit your tastes. I used another couple cloves of garlic because our household loves it. You could easily add chicken to this dish as well. Enjoy!"

Serving: 8 | Prep: 15 m | Cook: 20 m | Ready in: 45 m

Ingredients

- 1 (1 pound) package whole wheat penne pasta
- 1/3 cup olive oil
- 4 large cloves garlic, pressed
- 1 (8 ounce) jar marinated artichoke hearts, drained
- 7 pickled red peppers (such as Peppadew®), cut into strips
- 1/4 cup pitted Kalamata olives, quartered
- 2 cups fresh spinach leaves
- 1/2 cup crumbled feta cheese

Direction

- Fill a large pot with lightly salted water and bring to a boil. Stir in penne and return to a boil. Cook pasta uncovered, stirring occasionally, until cooked through but still firm to the bite, about 8 minutes; drain.
- Heat olive oil in a large nonstick skillet over medium heat and cook and stir garlic in the hot oil just until fragrant, about 30 seconds. Stir artichoke hearts, peppers, and olives into the skillet until flavors are blended, about 5 minutes. Gently fold the

spinach into the mixture and stir just until slightly wilted and dark green.
- Remove from heat and stir in penne pasta until thoroughly combined; lightly toss pasta mixture with feta cheese. Place a lid over the skillet and let the pasta and vegetables steam for 10 minutes before serving.

Nutrition Information

- Calories: 367 calories
- Total Fat: 14.7 g
- Cholesterol: 8 mg
- Sodium: 347 mg
- Total Carbohydrate: 47.4 g
- Protein: 12.9 g

127. MediterraneanStyle Eggplant Pasta

"A Mediterranean-style eggplant sauce for pasta that can be served with chicken for meat-lovers. Use good quality pasta, cheeses, and fresh herbs for best results. Serve with slivered or grated Parmesan. Serve with a green salad."

Serving: 4 | Prep: 10 m | Cook: 35 m | Ready in: 55 m

Ingredients

- 1 eggplant, cut into 3/4-inch slices
- salt as needed
- 9 ounces pappardelle pasta (wide fettuccine noodles)
- 3 tablespoons olive oil, divided
- 1 onion, finely chopped
- 3 cloves garlic, minced
- 2 teaspoons dried oregano
- 1 (18 ounce) can crushed tomatoes
- 1 tablespoon red wine vinegar
- 1 teaspoon salt
- 1 teaspoon white sugar
- 1/2 teaspoon freshly ground black pepper
- 1/2 pound fresh buffalo mozzarella cheese, torn into pieces
- 1/2 cup chopped fresh basil, or more to taste

Direction

- Arrange eggplant slices in a colander and sprinkle with enough salt to lightly coat; drain for about 10 minutes. Rinse eggplant and pat dry with paper towels. Chop eggplant into cubes.

- Bring a large pot of lightly salted water to a boil. Cook pappardelle at a boil until tender yet firm to the bite, about 10 to 11 minutes; drain.
- Heat 1 1/2 tablespoon olive oil in a skillet over medium heat; cook and stir eggplant, adding more oil if eggplant gets dry, until browned, 5 to 10 minutes. Transfer eggplant to a bowl, reserving oil in the skillet.
- Heat remaining oil in the same skillet; cook and stir onion and garlic until golden, about 10 minutes. Return eggplant to skillet and season with oregano; cook and stir for 1 minute more.
- Mix tomatoes, vinegar, salt, sugar, and black pepper into eggplant mixture; cover skillet and simmer sauce until eggplant is softened, about 10 minutes. Mix sauce with pasta in a bowl; top with mozzarella cheese and basil.

Nutrition Information

- Calories: 567 calories
- Total Fat: 24.4 g
- Cholesterol: 45 mg
- Sodium: 891 mg
- Total Carbohydrate: 68.1 g
- Protein: 21.9 g

128. Michelles Vegan Lasagna

"This tasty recipe is great for those who have a vegan or vegetarian diet or anyone wanting a healthier version of the old favorite.

I find it is plenty flavorful without soy cheese, but please add if your taste calls for it."

Serving: 6 | Prep: 15 m | Cook: 1 h | Ready in: 1 h 15 m

Ingredients

- 2 teaspoons vegetable oil
- 1/4 onion, finely chopped
- 1 green bell pepper, finely chopped
- 1 pound mushrooms, finely chopped
- 1 (14.5 ounce) can petite diced tomatoes
- 1 (14.5 ounce) can crushed tomatoes
- 1 (14 ounce) package firm tofu, drained and crumbled
- 1 (6 ounce) package baby spinach, coarsely chopped
- 2 cloves garlic, minced
- 1 teaspoon dried parsley
- 1 teaspoon dried basil
- 1 teaspoon dried oregano
- 1/4 teaspoon salt
- black pepper to taste
- 1 pinch red pepper flakes
- 1 (16 ounce) package lasagna noodles
- 1 (8 ounce) package shredded mozzarella-style vegan cheese (optional)
- 1/2 cup water

Direction

- Preheat oven to 400 degrees F (200 degrees C). Lightly oil a 9x13-inch baking dish.
- Heat oil in a large skillet over medium-high heat. Add onions and bell pepper; cook and stir until onion turns translucent and pepper begins to soften, 3 to 5 minutes. Add mushrooms; cook and stir until mushrooms soften, about 4 minutes.
- Stir diced tomatoes, crushed tomatoes, tofu, chopped spinach, garlic, parsley, basil, oregano, salt, pepper, and crushed pepper flakes into mushroom mixture. Bring to a simmer; reduce heat to medium-low and simmer sauce for 10 minutes.
- Pour a layer of the sauce into prepared baking dish. Cover with a layer of lasagna noodles. Add another layer of sauce and continue alternating layers of sauce and pasta, ending with sauce. Top with shredded cheese. Carefully add water. Cover baking dish with aluminum foil.
- Bake in preheated oven until pasta is fully cooked, about 40 minutes.

Nutrition Information

- Calories: 541 calories
- Total Fat: 17 g
- Cholesterol: 0 mg
- Sodium: 909 mg
- Total Carbohydrate: 72.9 g
- Protein: 24.5 g

129. Moms Baked Macaroni and Cheese

"Quick and easy -- macaroni, cheese soup, milk and Colby cheese!"

Serving: 6 | Prep: 5 m | Cook: 40 m | Ready in: 45 m

Ingredients

- 1 (16 ounce) package macaroni
- 1 (10.75 ounce) can condensed Cheddar cheese soup
- 1 cup milk
- 1 pound shredded Colby cheese

Direction

- Preheat oven to 350 degrees F (175 degrees C). Bring a large pot of lightly salted water to a boil. Add pasta and cook for 8 to 10 minutes or until al dente; drain.
- Place macaroni in a 2 quart casserole dish. Stir in cheese soup and milk until well combined. Sprinkle with shredded Colby.
- Bake 25 to 30 minutes, or until cheese is brown and bubbly.

Nutrition Information

- Calories: 674 calories
- Total Fat: 30.9 g
- Cholesterol: 87 mg
- Sodium: 849 mg
- Total Carbohydrate: 65.5 g
- Protein: 32.3 g

130. Moms Favorite Baked Mac and Cheese

"This is a macaroni and cheese I first made 3 years ago when I was in California. When I got back to Texas I made it for my mom. This is now her favorite baked macaroni and cheese. She begs me to make it when I come to visit."

Serving: 6 | Prep: 10 m | Cook: 45 m | Ready in: 1 h 5 m

Ingredients

- 2 tablespoons butter
- 1/4 cup finely chopped onion
- 2 tablespoons all-purpose flour
- 2 cups milk
- 3/4 teaspoon salt
- 1/2 teaspoon dry mustard
- 1/4 teaspoon ground black pepper
- 1 (8 ounce) package elbow macaroni
- 2 cups shredded sharp Cheddar cheese
- 1 (8 ounce) package processed American cheese, cut into strips

Direction

- Preheat oven to 350 degrees F (175 degrees C).
- Melt butter in a medium saucepan over medium heat. Sauté onion for 2 minutes. Stir in flour and cook 1 minute, stirring constantly. Stir in milk, salt, mustard and pepper; cook, stirring frequently, until mixture boils and thickens.
- Meanwhile, bring a pot of lightly salted water to a boil. Add macaroni and cook for 8 to 10 minutes or until al dente; drain.

- To the milk mixture add the Cheddar and American cheeses; stir until cheese melts. Combine macaroni and cheese sauce in a 2 quart baking dish; mix well.
- Bake in preheated oven for 30 minutes, or until hot and bubbly. Let cool 10 minutes before serving.

Nutrition Information

- Calories: 561 calories
- Total Fat: 33.3 g
- Cholesterol: 100 mg
- Sodium: 1194 mg
- Total Carbohydrate: 36.5 g
- Protein: 28.3 g

131. Moms Macaroni and Cheese

"Most recipes for macaroni and cheese use cheddar; this one uses American cheese. My mom learned to make this in Home Economics class in the 1930's and it has been a favorite in my family since then."

Serving: 8 | Cook: 30 m | Ready in: 30 m

Ingredients

- 1 pound elbow macaroni
- 1/2 cup vegetable oil
- 2 cups all-purpose flour
- 2 quarts milk
- 1/2 teaspoon ground black pepper
- 1 pound American cheese, cubed
- 1 (28 ounce) can crushed tomatoes
- 3/4 cup seasoned dry bread crumbs

Direction

- Preheat oven to 450 degrees F (230 degrees C). Bring a large pot of lightly salted water to a boil. Add pasta and cook for 5 to 7 minutes or until just less than al dente; drain.
- In large saucepan, heat oil over medium heat. Add flour all at once and stir vigorously until combined. Add milk a little at a time, stirring constantly until all milk is incorporated and sauce is smooth. Stir in pepper, American cheese and tomatoes. Stir until cheese is melted and mixture is smooth (if cheese starts to stick, reduce heat). Place macaroni in a 10x15 baking dish. Pour cheese mixture over macaroni, and sprinkle with bread crumbs.

- Bake 15 minutes, or until top is golden.

Nutrition Information

- Calories: 869 calories
- Total Fat: 38.8 g
- Cholesterol: 73 mg
- Sodium: 1274 mg
- Total Carbohydrate: 94.9 g
- Protein: 35.3 g

132. Moms Peas and Noodles

"This was a dish my mother made during Lent when we were kids and at other times to stretch our grocery dollars. It's easy to make and simple in taste. This recipe can be multiplied easily to serve the number of people eating."

Serving: 1 | Prep: 10 m | Cook: 15 m | Ready in: 25 m

Ingredients

- 1 cup uncooked whole-wheat pasta shells
- 1/3 cup frozen peas
- 2 eggs, beaten
- 2 tablespoons grated Parmesan cheese
- 1/4 teaspoon ground black pepper
- 1 teaspoon grated Parmesan cheese

Direction

- Fill a saucepan with lightly salted water and bring to a rolling boil over high heat. Once the water is boiling, stir in the shell pasta, and return to a boil. Cook the pasta uncovered, stirring occasionally, until the pasta has cooked through, but is still firm to the bite, about 10 minutes. Stir in the frozen peas, and cook for 1 more minute; drain well in a colander set in the sink. Return the pasta and peas to the saucepan.
- Mix in the eggs, 2 tablespoons of Parmesan cheese, and black pepper; cook over low heat, stirring constantly, until the eggs are cooked through, 2 to 3 minutes. Serve sprinkled with 1 teaspoon of Parmesan cheese.

Nutrition Information

- Calories: 434 calories
- Total Fat: 14.4 g
- Cholesterol: 383 mg
- Sodium: 386 mg
- Total Carbohydrate: 51.3 g
- Protein: 28.3 g

133. Monterey Spaghetti

"Using a slow cooker makes this recipe easy to prepare. Healthy and wholesome, too!"

Serving: 8

Ingredients

- 4 ounces spaghetti, broken into pieces
- 1 egg
- 1 cup sour cream
- 1/4 cup grated Parmesan cheese
- 1/8 teaspoon crushed garlic
- 3 cups shredded Monterey Jack cheese
- 1 (10 ounce) package frozen chopped spinach, thawed and drained
- 1/2 (6 ounce) can French fried onions

Direction

- In a large pot with boiling salted water cook spaghetti until al dente. Drain.
- In a large bowl mix together the sour cream, grated Parmesan cheese, and minced garlic. After beating the egg in a small bowl, transfer to the large bowl and blend together. Transfer to a greased slow cooker.
- Mix cooked and drained spaghetti, 2 cups grated Monterey Jack cheese, thawed spinach, and half of the French fried onions to the slow cooker. Stir contents of slow cooker until just blended.

- Cover and cook on low for 6 to 8 hours or high heat for 3 to 4 hours.
- In last 30 minutes of cooking, turn to high if cooking on low and add remainder of grated Monterey Jack cheese and French fried onions to top of casserole. Serve when cheese is melted.

Nutrition Information

- Calories: 369 calories
- Total Fat: 25.9 g
- Cholesterol: 76 mg
- Sodium: 406 mg
- Total Carbohydrate: 18.1 g
- Protein: 16.1 g

134. Mostaccioli with Spinach and Feta

"I use mostaccioli or penne, whichever is available. I have served this hot or cold."

Serving: 6 | Prep: 20 m | Cook: 10 m | Ready in: 30 m

Ingredients

- 8 ounces penne pasta
- 2 tablespoons olive oil
- 3 cups chopped tomatoes
- 10 ounces fresh spinach, washed and chopped
- 1 clove garlic, minced
- 8 ounces tomato basil feta cheese
- salt to taste
- ground black pepper to taste

Direction

- Cook pasta according to package directions. Drain, and set aside.
- Heat oil in a large pot. Add tomatoes, spinach, and garlic; cook and stir 2 minutes, or until spinach is wilted and mixture is thoroughly heated. Add pasta and cheese; cook 1 minute. Season to taste with salt and pepper.

Nutrition Information

- Calories: 301 calories
- Total Fat: 13.8 g

- Cholesterol: 34 mg
- Sodium: 465 mg
- Total Carbohydrate: 34.1 g
- Protein: 12.5 g

135. Mushroom and Spinach Ravioli with Chive Butter Sauce

"This homemade ravioli is actually vegetarian, although no one who tries it can tell! The savory filling contains three different cheeses, mushrooms, and spinach. Although it's a rather time-consuming recipe to prepare, the results are well worth it!"

Serving: 6 | Prep: 2 h | Cook: 20 m | Ready in: 2 h 20 m

Ingredients

- 1 teaspoon olive oil
- 1 1/2 tablespoons water, or more if needed
- 2 eggs
- 2 cups all-purpose flour, or more if needed
- 1/4 teaspoon salt
- 1 teaspoon olive oil
- 1 clove garlic, minced
- 1/2 cup chopped onion
- 1 (8 ounce) package fresh mushrooms, coarsely chopped
- 4 ounces cream cheese, softened
- 1/3 cup grated Parmesan cheese
- 1/2 cup mozzarella cheese
- 1/2 cup frozen chopped spinach, thawed and drained
- 1 tablespoon chopped fresh chives
- 1 tablespoon chopped fresh parsley
- 1/2 teaspoon ground cayenne pepper
- salt and ground black pepper to taste
- 1 egg white, beaten
- 3 tablespoons butter
- 1 1/2 teaspoons chopped fresh chives

Direction

- Whisk together 1 teaspoon olive oil, water, and whole eggs in a bowl until evenly blended; set aside. Combine flour and salt in a separate large bowl, and make a well in the center. Pour the egg mixture into the well and stir just until combined. Turn dough out onto a lightly floured surface and knead until smooth, 5 to 10 minutes, adding more flour or water as needed. Wrap dough tightly with plastic wrap, and set aside to rest.
- Heat 1 teaspoon olive oil in a skillet over medium heat. Stir in the garlic and onion; cook and stir until the onion begins to soften, about 2 minutes. Add the mushrooms, and continue cooking and stirring until the vegetables are soft and the liquid has evaporated, about 10 minutes. Remove from heat, and allow to cool.
- Beat cream cheese in a bowl until smooth. Stir in the cooled mushroom mixture, Parmesan cheese, mozzarella cheese, spinach, 1 tablespoon chives, parsley, and cayenne pepper. Season with salt and pepper.
- Roll the pasta dough out to about 1/16 inch thick. Cut 3 to 4-inch circles using a large cookie cutter. Roll each circle out as thin as possible. Working with one circle at a time, brush the pasta lightly with the egg white. Scoop about 1 heaping tablespoon full of the mushroom filling onto the center of the pasta, then cover with a second piece of pasta, pinching the edges to seal. Cut the sealed ravioli with the cookie cutter once more to create a uniform shape. Place the finished ravioli on a floured baking sheet, and repeat the process with the remaining pasta and filling.
- Fill a large pot with lightly salted water and bring to a rolling boil over high heat. Once the water is boiling, stir in the ravioli and return to a boil. Cook until the pasta floats to the top, 3 to 4 minutes; drain.

- To make sauce: Melt butter in a skillet over high heat, cooking and stirring until browned, 5 to 7 minutes. Stir in 1 1/2 teaspoons chives. Serve over hot ravioli.

Nutrition Information

- Calories: 371 calories
- Total Fat: 19 g
- Cholesterol: 108 mg
- Sodium: 392 mg
- Total Carbohydrate: 36.3 g
- Protein: 14.4 g

136. Mushroom Kale and Bok Choy Ramen

"This ramen bowl with mushrooms, kale, carrots, and bok choy, is a quick, easy lo mein substitute."

Serving: 4 | Prep: 25 m | Cook: 10 m | Ready in: 35 m

Ingredients

- 3 (3 ounce) packages instant ramen noodles (without flavor packet)
- 2 1/2 cups boiling water
- 3 tablespoons soy sauce
- 3 tablespoons balsamic vinegar
- 2 teaspoons sesame oil
- 1 teaspoon white sugar
- 1 teaspoon minced garlic, or to taste
- 1/4 teaspoon ground ginger
- 2 teaspoons vegetable oil
- 2 cups chopped baby bok choy
- 1/2 medium onion, chopped
- 1/3 cup chopped carrots
- 1/2 cup chopped cremini mushrooms
- 1/2 cup chopped shiitake mushrooms
- 1/2 cup chopped kale

Direction

- Place ramen bricks in a shallow heat-safe bowl. Pour boiling water over ramen and let stand until noodles start to separate

and soften.
- Mix soy sauce, balsamic vinegar, sesame oil, sugar, garlic, and ginger together in a small bowl or glass jar.
- Heat vegetable oil in a large skillet or wok over medium-high heat. Sauté bok choy, onion, and carrots until onion is translucent, 3 to 5 minutes. Add cremini mushrooms, shiitake mushrooms, and kale. Sauté until kale begins to wilt, 3 to 5 minutes.
- Separate ramen noodles with a fork and drain any excess water. Add drained noodles to the skillet and increase heat to high. Pour soy and vinegar sauce over the noodles and vegetables. Stir until flavors combine, about 2 minutes.

Nutrition Information

- Calories: 358 calories
- Total Fat: 15.3 g
- Cholesterol: 0 mg
- Sodium: 1010 mg
- Total Carbohydrate: 46.4 g
- Protein: 8.7 g

137. Mushroom Spinach Mac and Cheese

"Tofu adds a creamy texture to this healthy spin on Macaroni and Cheese! Great for a side dish or as a meal by itself. Top with bread crumbs, crushed crackers, or cereal before baking if desired."

Serving: 6 | Prep: 25 m | Cook: 50 m | Ready in: 1 h 15 m

Ingredients

- 1 (16 ounce) package elbow macaroni
- 1 (12 ounce) package soft silken tofu
- 8 ounces shredded Swiss cheese
- 1/2 cup Greek yogurt
- 1 teaspoon Dijon mustard
- 1 tablespoon olive oil
- 8 ounces portobello mushrooms, stemmed and sliced
- 1 cup frozen spinach, thawed
- 1 green bell pepper, chopped
- 1 onion, diced
- 2 cloves garlic, minced
- salt and ground black pepper to taste

Direction

- Bring a large pot of lightly salted water to a boil. Cook elbow macaroni in the boiling water, stirring occasionally until tender yet firm to the bite, 8 minutes. Drain and transfer to a 9x13-inch casserole dish.
- Preheat oven to 350 degrees F (175 degrees C).

- Blend tofu in a food processor until smooth, about 2 minutes. Add Swiss cheese, Greek yogurt, and Dijon mustard; mix well to combine.
- Heat oil in a large skillet over medium-high heat. Add mushrooms, spinach, green bell pepper, onion, and garlic; sauté until tender, about 5 minutes. Stir tofu mixture into the skillet. Cook until flavors combine, 2 to 3 minutes. Season with salt and ground black pepper.
- Spoon tofu and mushroom mixture over macaroni in the casserole dish; mix to combine. Cover with aluminum foil.
- Bake in the preheated oven until bubbly and golden, about 30 minutes.

Nutrition Information

- Calories: 524 calories
- Total Fat: 17.3 g
- Cholesterol: 39 mg
- Sodium: 160 mg
- Total Carbohydrate: 66.2 g
- Protein: 25.9 g

138. NoCream Pasta Primavera

"Spring veggies benefit from a quick roasting in olive oil and herbs before being tossed with penne. No cream here, just the fresh flavors of olive oil, balsamic vinegar, and lemon. A beautiful dish."

Serving: 6 | Prep: 25 m | Cook: 35 m | Ready in: 1 h

Ingredients

- 1 (12 ounce) package penne pasta
- 1 yellow squash, chopped
- 1 zucchini, chopped
- 1 carrot, cut into matchsticks
- 1/2 red bell peppers, cut into matchsticks
- 1/2 pint grape tomatoes
- 1 cup fresh green beans, trimmed and cut into 1 inch pieces
- 5 spears asparagus, trimmed and cut into 1 inch pieces
- 1/4 cup olive oil, divided
- 1 tablespoon Italian seasoning
- 1/2 tablespoon lemon juice
- 1/4 teaspoon salt
- 1/4 teaspoon coarsely ground black pepper
- 1 tablespoon butter
- 1/4 large yellow onion, thinly sliced
- 2 cloves garlic, thinly sliced
- 2 teaspoons lemon zest
- 1/3 cup chopped fresh basil leaves
- 1/3 cup chopped fresh parsley
- 3 tablespoons balsamic vinegar
- 1/2 cup grated Romano cheese

Direction

- Preheat oven to 450 degrees F (230 degrees C). Line a baking sheet with aluminum foil.
- Bring a large pot of lightly salted water to a boil. Add penne pasta and cook until tender yet firm to the bite, 10 to 12 minutes; drain.
- Toss squash, zucchini, carrot, red bell pepper, tomatoes, green beans, and asparagus together in a bowl with 2 tablespoons olive oil, salt, pepper, lemon juice, and Italian seasoning. Arrange vegetables on the lined baking sheet.
- Roast vegetables in preheated oven until tender, about 15 minutes.
- Heat remaining olive oil and butter in a large skillet. Cook onion and garlic in hot oil until tender, 5 to 7 minutes. Mix cooked pasta, lemon zest, basil, parsley, and balsamic vinegar into the onion mixture. Gently toss and cook until heated through, 3 to 5 minutes. Remove from heat and transfer to a large bowl. Toss with roasted vegetables and sprinkle with Romano cheese.

Nutrition Information

- Calories: 406 calories
- Total Fat: 15.4 g
- Cholesterol: 15 mg
- Sodium: 252 mg
- Total Carbohydrate: 54.4 g
- Protein: 13.6 g

139. Old Fashioned Mac and Cheese

"This is a classic recipe for macaroni and cheese. The kids will love this!"

Serving: 7 | Prep: 20 m | Cook: 45 m | Ready in: 1 h 5 m

Ingredients

- 2 cups uncooked elbow macaroni
- 4 tablespoons butter
- 2 tablespoons all-purpose flour
- 2 cups milk
- 1/4 onion, minced
- salt and pepper to taste
- 1/4 pound processed cheese food
- 1/4 pound shredded Cheddar cheese
- 1/4 pound shredded Swiss cheese

Direction

- Preheat oven to 350 degrees F (175 degrees C).
- Prepare the elbow macaroni according to package directions.
- Meanwhile, melt the butter in a small saucepan over medium high heat. Stir in the flour until a cream colored paste forms. Then pour in the milk and stir constantly until this comes to a hard boil, then stir for 1 more minute. Remove from heat and set aside.
- When the macaroni is cooked, spread 1/2 of it into the bottom of a lightly greased 9x13-inch baking dish. Then layer 1/2 of the grated onion, 1/2 of the salt and pepper and 1/2 of each of the

cheeses. Repeat this one more time: macaroni, onion, salt and pepper and cheeses, and then pour the reserved white sauce over all. Top off with small pats of butter to taste.
- Cover and bake at 350 degrees F (175 degrees C) for 45 minutes.

Nutrition Information

- Calories: 401 calories
- Total Fat: 23.3 g
- Cholesterol: 70 mg
- Sodium: 450 mg
- Total Carbohydrate: 29.1 g
- Protein: 18.5 g

140. Olive and Feta Pasta

"I whipped up this pasta dish to satisfy a craving for olives and feta cheese. Add artichokes or spinach for variation."

Serving: 4 | Prep: 15 m | Cook: 20 m | Ready in: 35 m

Ingredients

- 8 ounces uncooked whole wheat spaghetti
- 1 tablespoon olive oil
- 2 cloves garlic, minced
- 8 ounces crimini mushrooms, sliced
- 2 small zucchini, sliced
- dried oregano to taste
- salt and pepper to taste
- 12 black olives, pitted and sliced
- 1 ounce crumbled feta cheese

Direction

- Bring a large pot of lightly salted water to a boil. Add spaghetti and cook for 8 to 10 minutes or until al dente; drain.
- Heat the olive oil in a skillet over medium heat, and sauté the garlic 2 minutes. Mix in mushrooms and zucchini. Season with oregano, salt, and pepper. Stir in olives, and cook until heated through. Place pasta in the skillet, toss to coat, and continue cooking about 2 minutes. Top with feta cheese to serve.

Nutrition Information

- Calories: 274 calories

- Total Fat: 7.4 g
- Cholesterol: 6 mg
- Sodium: 242 mg
- Total Carbohydrate: 43.5 g
- Protein: 12.1 g

141. Orzo and Potato Parmesan

"This is a great recipe for people on a budget or for picky eaters. It is also very easy to make. This recipe lists the basic ingredients, but you should try adding other vegetables or ingredients to suit your taste. I typically add carrots and onions. Just be sure to add a little extra water to compensate for additional ingredients. If you aren't a vegetarian you can use chicken bouillon."

Serving: 4 | Prep: 15 m | Cook: 12 m | Ready in: 30 m

Ingredients

- 2 tablespoons butter
- 1 cup uncooked orzo pasta
- 2 teaspoons minced garlic
- 2 potatoes, peeled and diced
- 1 carrot, sliced
- 1 onion, chopped
- 1 teaspoon dried Italian seasoning
- salt and pepper to taste
- 3 cups water
- 1 cube vegetable bouillon
- 1 cup freshly grated Parmesan cheese

Direction

- Melt butter in a medium saucepan over medium heat. Stir in orzo and garlic, and sauté until lightly browned. Place potatoes, carrot, and onion in the saucepan. Continue to cook and stir until tender. Season with dried Italian seasoning, salt, and pepper.
- Mix water into the saucepan. Stir in vegetable bouillon until dissolved. Cover, reduce heat, and simmer 12 minutes, or until

orzo is tender and most of the liquid has been absorbed. Top with Parmesan cheese to serve.

Nutrition Information

- Calories: 465 calories
- Total Fat: 13.9 g
- Cholesterol: 37 mg
- Sodium: 452 mg
- Total Carbohydrate: 66.1 g
- Protein: 20 g

142. Orzo with SunDried Tomatoes and Kalamata Olives

"A favorite side dish for Italian meals that is hearty enough to stand alone as a vegetarian main dish. Can be served warm or chilled for later."

Serving: 2 | Prep: 10 m | Cook: 15 m | Ready in: 25 m

Ingredients

- 2/3 cup orzo pasta
- 1/2 cup chopped sun-dried tomatoes
- 1/2 cup pitted kalamata olives
- 1/2 cup pesto
- 1/2 cup grated Parmesan cheese
- 1 tablespoon olive oil, or to taste

Direction

- Bring a large pot of lightly salted water to a boil. Cook orzo in the boiling water, stirring occasionally until cooked through but firm to the bite, about 11 minutes. Drain.
- Mix orzo pasta, tomatoes, and olives together in a large bowl. Pour pesto over pasta mixture and stir to coat. Sprinkle Parmesan cheese over the pasta mixture; stir. Drizzle olive oil over the salad and stir to achieve your preferred moisture level.

Nutrition Information

- Calories: 828 calories
- Total Fat: 51.1 g

- Cholesterol: 38 mg
- Sodium: 1618 mg
- Total Carbohydrate: 65.2 g
- Protein: 30.4 g

143. Oyster Mushroom Pasta

"This is so easy and so delicious. Oyster mushrooms are poached in butter and cream and tossed with pasta, Parmesan cheese and green onions. Mmmmmmmm!"

Serving: 4 | Prep: 15 m | Cook: 30 m | Ready in: 45 m

Ingredients

- 1 (16 ounce) package linguine pasta
- 1/2 cup butter
- 1 pound oyster mushrooms, chopped
- 1/3 cup chopped fresh parsley
- salt and ground black pepper to taste
- 2/3 cup heavy whipping cream
- 4 green onions, chopped
- 1/4 cup Parmesan cheese

Direction

- Bring a large pot of lightly salted water to a boil. Cook linguine at a boil until tender yet firm to the bite, about 11 minutes. Drain and transfer to a serving bowl.
- Melt butter in a large skillet over medium heat. Add mushrooms; cook and stir until tender and lightly browned, about 5 minutes. Stir in parsley, salt, and black pepper; cook until flavors combine, about 1 minute. Pour in heavy cream. Bring to a gentle boil; cook until sauce thickens slightly, about 5 minutes.
- Pour sauce over pasta in the serving bowl; toss to combine. Add green onions and Parmesan cheese; toss until combined.

Nutrition Information

- Calories: 819 calories
- Total Fat: 42.2 g
- Cholesterol: 120 mg
- Sodium: 325 mg
- Total Carbohydrate: 91.6 g
- Protein: 22.1 g

144. Pad Thai

"This is a non-spicy, vegetarian version of the traditional Thai cellophane noodle dish. Serve on its own for a quick meal, or with a variety of curries for a more elaborate occasion."

Serving: 4 | Prep: 15 m | Cook: 10 m | Ready in: 25 m

Ingredients

- 1 (6.75 ounce) package thin rice noodles
- 2 tablespoons vegetable oil
- 3 ounces fried tofu, sliced into thin strips
- 1 clove garlic, minced
- 1 egg
- 1 tablespoon soy sauce
- 1 pinch white sugar
- 2 tablespoons chopped peanuts
- 1 cup fresh bean sprouts
- 1 tablespoon chopped fresh cilantro
- 1 lime, cut into wedges

Direction

- Place noodles in a heatproof bowl and cover with boiling water. Allow to soak for 5 minutes, until pliable but not mushy. Drain water and set aside.
- Heat oil in wok over medium heat. Add garlic, and fry until brown. Add noodles, and fry until heated through. Push to the side.
- Break egg into the base of the wok, and mix gently. As it begins to set, break it up and mix it into the noodles. Mix in soy sauce

and sugar. Stir in tofu, bean sprouts, peanuts, and cilantro. Remove from heat. Garnish with lime wedges.

Nutrition Information

- Calories: 352 calories
- Total Fat: 15 g
- Cholesterol: 46 mg
- Sodium: 335 mg
- Total Carbohydrate: 46.8 g
- Protein: 9.2 g

145. Pad Thai with Tofu

"This is a favorite Thai dish that is light and combines sour, salt, sweet, and spicy flavors."

Serving: 4 | Prep: 20 m | Cook: 15 m | Ready in: 45 m

Ingredients

- 1 (12 ounce) package tofu, drained and cubed
- 1 tablespoon cornstarch
- 3 tablespoons vegetable oil, divided
- 8 ounces dry rice stick noodles
- Sauce:
- 1/4 cup water
- 1/4 cup sriracha hot sauce
- 1/4 cup soy sauce
- 2 tablespoons white sugar
- 1 tablespoon tamarind concentrate
- 1 teaspoon red pepper flakes
- 1/2 onion, sliced
- 1 egg (optional)
- 2 tablespoons chopped spring onions
- 1 tablespoon crushed peanuts
- 1 lime, cut into wedges

Direction

- Coat tofu with cornstarch in a bowl. Heat 2 tablespoons vegetable oil in a wok or large skillet over medium heat; fry tofu until lightly browned on all sides, 1 to 2 minutes per side.

- Place noodles in a bowl and pour in enough boiling water to cover; soak until softened, about 3 minutes. Drain.
- Combine water, sriracha, soy sauce, sugar, tamarind concentrate, and red pepper flakes in a saucepan over low heat. Cook and stir sauce until flavors blend, about 5 minutes.
- Heat 1 tablespoon vegetable oil in a wok over medium-high heat. Add tofu, noodles, and sliced onion; cook and stir until tofu is golden brown; about 3 minutes. Stir in sauce gradually until noodles are well-coated.
- Push noodle mixture to one side of the wok. Crack egg onto opposite side of wok; stir until beginning to set, 30 seconds to 1 minute. Stir egg into noodles gently. Garnish with green onions, peanuts, and lime wedges.

Nutrition Information

- Calories: 452 calories
- Total Fat: 16.8 g
- Cholesterol: 46 mg
- Sodium: 1579 mg
- Total Carbohydrate: 61.1 g
- Protein: 14.4 g

146. Pasta and Bean Casserole

"An easy do-ahead dish perfect for potlucks and dinner parties. This hearty and flavorful vegetarian dish can easily be made vegan and will satisfy everyone."

Serving: 6 | Prep: 25 m | Cook: 50 m | Ready in: 1 h 15 m

Ingredients

- 1 (16 ounce) package seashell pasta
- 2 tablespoons olive oil
- 1 medium onion, peeled and diced
- 3 cloves garlic, minced
- 1/2 green bell pepper, chopped
- 1/2 red bell pepper, chopped
- 1 jalapeno pepper, minced (optional)
- 1 (14.5 ounce) can diced tomatoes with juice
- 1 (15 ounce) can garbanzo beans
- 1 teaspoon basil
- 1 teaspoon dried oregano
- 1 teaspoon ground paprika
- 1 teaspoon ground cumin
- 1 teaspoon ground coriander
- salt to taste
- black pepper to taste
- 1/2 cup shredded mozzarella cheese

Direction

- Preheat oven to 350 degrees F (175 degrees C). Oil a 9x13 inch baking dish.

- Bring a large pot of lightly salted water to a boil. Cook pasta in boiling water for 8 to 10 minutes, or until al dente. Drain.
- Heat olive oil in a skillet over medium heat. Cook onion in oil until soft, then add garlic and red and green peppers. Stir in jalapeno, if desired. Continue cooking for 2 more minutes. Stir in tomatoes and garbanzo beans. Season with basil, oregano, paprika, cumin, coriander, and salt and pepper. Simmer with 5 minutes. Remove from heat, and stir in pasta. Transfer to prepared baking dish, and top with cheese.
- Bake in preheated oven for 30 to 40 minutes, or until cheese is melted and bubbly.

Nutrition Information

- Calories: 422 calories
- Total Fat: 8.6 g
- Cholesterol: 6 mg
- Sodium: 504 mg
- Total Carbohydrate: 71.7 g
- Protein: 15.8 g

147. Pasta and Vegetable Saute

"A colorful and tasty presentation."

Serving: 5

Ingredients

- 1/2 cup olive oil
- 1 onion, thinly sliced
- 1 red bell pepper, thinly sliced
- 1 green bell pepper, sliced
- 1 carrot, sliced
- 1/2 cup chopped green onions
- 2 cloves garlic, minced
- 1 (5.5 ounce) can baby corn, drained
- 1 (4.5 ounce) can mushrooms, drained
- 1 teaspoon dried parsley
- 1/4 teaspoon garlic powder
- salt and pepper to taste
- 2 tablespoons grated Parmesan cheese
- 1 pound uncooked pasta

Direction

- Heat olive oil in large saucepan. Add onion, peppers and carrot and sauté until onion is golden. Stir in the scallions and minced garlic and sauté for 2 minutes. Stir in the baby corn, mushroom and seasonings and heat through.
- Toss the cooked pasta with the vegetables and top with parmesan cheese, if desired.

Nutrition Information

- Calories: 505 calories
- Total Fat: 24.5 g
- Cholesterol: 68 mg
- Sodium: 187 mg
- Total Carbohydrate: 59.4 g
- Protein: 12.6 g

148. Pasta and White Beans Gratin

"If you first cook the pasta, and then use the same pot to cook the beans, you will only need one pot and a casserole dish to make this meal. To save time, cook the pasta and the beans in different pots at the same time, and use prepared pesto instead of fresh basil and Parmesan."

Serving: 8 | Prep: 20 m | Cook: 50 m | Ready in: 1 h 10 m

Ingredients

- 2 cups uncooked pasta shells
- 2 cups loosely packed fresh basil
- 3 cloves garlic
- 1 cup grated Parmesan cheese
- 1 teaspoon olive oil
- 1 cup ricotta cheese
- 1/2 cup chopped onion
- 3 sprigs fresh thyme
- 1 bay leaf
- 1 tablespoon olive oil
- 2 (15 ounce) cans white beans
- 1 tablespoon balsamic vinegar
- salt and pepper to taste
- 2 tomatoes, chopped
- 1/2 cup bread crumbs
- 1 tablespoon olive oil

Direction

- Bring a large pot of water to a boil. Cook pasta in boiling water until done. Drain, and set aside. Meanwhile mince basil and

garlic with Parmesan cheese. Transfer to a medium bowl, and mix with 1 teaspoon olive oil. Mix in ricotta.
- In a saucepan, cook onions with thyme and bay leaf in 1 tablespoon olive oil. Stir in beans and balsamic vinegar, and simmer for 20 minutes. Season to taste with salt and pepper.
- Preheat oven to 350 degrees F (175 degrees C). Combine beans, tomatoes, and pasta in a well-oiled 2 quart casserole dish. Place spoonfuls of the ricotta mixture in the pasta and beans, and press down to cover. In a small bowl, moisten bread crumbs with 1 tablespoon olive oil, and sprinkle over casserole.
- Bake in preheated oven for 30 minutes, or until hot and bubbly.

Nutrition Information

- Calories: 351 calories
- Total Fat: 9 g
- Cholesterol: 11 mg
- Sodium: 398 mg
- Total Carbohydrate: 51.2 g
- Protein: 17.9 g

149. Pasta Carcione

"Bow tie pasta tossed with spinach, tomatoes, goat cheese and olive oil. This is the best pasta recipe in the world! I made it up one day instead of serving a heavy pasta dish. The goat cheese makes this recipe!"

Serving: 5 | Prep: 20 m | Cook: 15 m | Ready in: 35 m

Ingredients

- 10 ounces spinach, rinsed
- 1 (16 ounce) package bow tie pasta
- 1/4 cup olive oil
- salt and pepper to taste
- 2 1/2 cups cherry tomatoes, quartered
- 8 ounces crumbled goat cheese

Direction

- Remove stems from spinach and stack leaves together; chop thin longer strips instead of square chops and set aside.
- Bring a large pot of lightly salted water to a boil. Add pasta and cook for 8 to 10 minutes or until al dente; drain and place in a large bowl.
- Drizzle olive oil over pasta and add salt and pepper to taste, spinach and tomatoes; gently toss.
- Add goat cheese and serve warm or room temperature.

Nutrition Information

- Calories: 610 calories
- Total Fat: 26.9 g

- Cholesterol: 36 mg
- Sodium: 289 mg
- Total Carbohydrate: 71.9 g
- Protein: 23.9 g

150. Pasta Pascal

"Named after the friend that first introduced this dish to me one homesick day. It is a simple pasta that lends itself to endless variety. Try adding mushrooms or zucchini. I find that angel hair pasta is best, but thicker pasta will certainly work as well. Drizzle with extra olive oil before serving."

Serving: 4 | Prep: 10 m | Cook: 15 m | Ready in: 25 m

Ingredients

- 5 tablespoons olive oil
- 4 cloves garlic, minced
- 1 onion, chopped
- 4 roma (plum) tomatoes, diced
- 1/2 teaspoon dried oregano
- 1/2 teaspoon dried basil
- salt and pepper to taste
- 1 pound angel hair pasta

Direction

- In a medium skillet over medium-high heat, sauté garlic in oil 1 to 2 minutes. Stir in onion and cook 2 minutes more. Stir in tomatoes, oregano, basil, salt and pepper. Reduce heat to medium-low and let simmer.
- Bring a large pot of lightly salted water to a boil. Add pasta and cook for 3 to 5 minutes or until al dente; drain.
- Toss hot pasta with tomato mixture. Serve.

Nutrition Information

- Calories: 497 calories
- Total Fat: 20.1 g
- Cholesterol: 0 mg
- Sodium: 235 mg
- Total Carbohydrate: 68.1 g
- Protein: 13.1 g

151. Pasta Shells Florentine

"Large pasta shells stuffed with lowfat cheeses and spinach, smothered in marinara sauce and baked. You can use 2 tablespoons egg substitute in place of the egg white if you prefer. Lighten it up even more by using nonfat cottage cheese."

Serving: 4

Ingredients

- 16 jumbo pasta shells
- 1 (10 ounce) package frozen chopped spinach, thawed and drained
- 6 ounces low fat mozzarella cheese, shredded
- 1 cup low-fat cottage cheese
- 1 egg white
- 1 tablespoon grated Parmesan cheese
- 1/4 teaspoon ground nutmeg
- 2 tablespoons Italian seasoning
- 1 (16 ounce) jar spaghetti sauce

Direction

- In a large pot of salted water boil pasta shells until al dente. Drain well and rinse.
- Preheat oven to 375 degrees F (175 degrees C).
- In medium bowl, combine spinach, mozzarella cheese, cottage cheese, egg white, parmesan cheese, nutmeg, and Italian seasoning until blended.
- Fill each pasta shell with a heaping tablespoon of spinach mixture. Pour 1 cup spaghetti sauce into an 8x12 inch baking

dish, spread evenly. Place shells in pan. Spoon remaining spaghetti sauce over shells. Cover with aluminum foil and bake for 30 to 40 minutes, or until shells are heated through.

Nutrition Information

- Calories: 539 calories
- Total Fat: 12.2 g
- Cholesterol: 30 mg
- Sodium: 1078 mg
- Total Carbohydrate: 73.4 g
- Protein: 34.7 g

152. Pasta Shells with Portobello Mushrooms and Asparagus in Boursin Sauce

"From my friend Tasneem - an easy recipe to prepare, resulting in a downright sophisticated dish. Asparagus and pasta are tossed with a cheesy mushroom sauce."

Serving: 6 | Prep: 15 m | Cook: 25 m | Ready in: 40 m

Ingredients

- 1 tablespoon butter
- 1 tablespoon olive oil
- 1 pound portobello mushrooms, stems removed
- 1/2 teaspoon salt
- 1 1/4 cups low-sodium chicken broth
- 1 (5.2 ounce) package pepper Boursin cheese
- 3/4 pound uncooked pasta shells
- 1 pound fresh asparagus, trimmed

Direction

- In a large skillet over medium heat, melt the butter and heat the olive oil. Cut the mushroom caps in half, and slice 1/4 inch thick. Cook mushrooms in the skillet 8 minutes, or until tender and lightly browned. Season with salt. Stir in the chicken broth and Boursin cheese. Reduce heat and simmer, stirring constantly, until well blended.
- Bring a large pot of lightly salted water to a boil. Add shell pasta and cook for 5 minutes. Place the asparagus into the pot, and

continue cooking 5 minutes, until the pasta is al dente and the asparagus is tender; drain. Toss with the mushroom sauce to serve.

Nutrition Information

- Calories: 400 calories
- Total Fat: 16.6 g
- Cholesterol: 35 mg
- Sodium: 388 mg
- Total Carbohydrate: 51.6 g
- Protein: 14.1 g

153. Pasta Siciliano

"This wonderful and easy skillet pasta dish includes sun-dried tomatoes, olives, pine nuts, feta cheese, and crushed red pepper flakes. This is an authentic alternative that gets rave reviews in our family."

Serving: 8 | Prep: 15 m | Cook: 20 m | Ready in: 35 m

Ingredients

- 1 (16 ounce) package uncooked farfalle pasta
- 1/4 cup olive oil
- 3 cloves chopped garlic
- 1 teaspoon crushed red pepper flakes
- 2 tablespoons lemon juice
- 1/2 cup pine nuts
- 1 (2.25 ounce) can sliced black olives
- 1/2 cup chopped sun-dried tomatoes
- 1 cup crumbled feta cheese
- salt and pepper to taste

Direction

- Bring a large pot of lightly salted water to a boil. Place farfalle pasta in the pot, cook for 8 to 10 minutes, until al dente, and drain.
- Heat the oil in a large skillet over medium heat, and cook the garlic until lightly browned. Mix in red pepper and lemon juice. Stir in the pine nuts, olives, and sun-dried tomatoes. Toss in the cooked pasta and feta cheese. Season with salt and pepper.

Nutrition Information

- Calories: 434 calories
- Total Fat: 20.1 g
- Cholesterol: 28 mg
- Sodium: 639 mg
- Total Carbohydrate: 49 g
- Protein: 15.3 g

154. Pasta with Arugula and Tomatoes

"This is a super-simple, quick pasta recipe that tastes best with cherry tomatoes or other sun-ripened tomatoes. It is perfect during the summer months when tomatoes are in season."

Serving: 3 | Prep: 5 m | Cook: 20 m | Ready in: 25 m

Ingredients

- 10 ounces spaghetti
- 4 tablespoons olive oil
- 2 cloves garlic, minced
- 1 pint cherry tomatoes, halved
- salt and freshly ground black pepper to taste
- 1 (5 ounce) package arugula, torn
- 2 tablespoons shaved Parmesan cheese, or more to taste

Direction

- Bring a large pot of lightly salted water to a boil. Cook spaghetti in the boiling water, stirring occasionally, until tender yet firm to the bite, about 12 minutes. Drain.
- Meanwhile, heat olive oil in a skillet over medium-low heat and cook garlic until translucent and fragrant, about 2 minutes. Add cherry tomatoes. Increase heat, cook, and stir until lightly browned, 5 to 7 minutes. Season with salt and pepper.
- Remove skillet from heat and mix in arugula. Mix in cooked spaghetti and drizzle with olive oil. Serve immediately with Parmesan cheese.

Nutrition Information

- Calories: 555 calories
- Total Fat: 21 g
- Cholesterol: 3 mg
- Sodium: 130 mg
- Total Carbohydrate: 76.8 g
- Protein: 15.6 g

155. Pasta with Arugula Pesto

"The unique flavour of arugula makes this pesto peppery and robust."

Serving: 8 | Prep: 25 m | Ready in: 25 m

Ingredients

- 1/4 cup chopped walnuts
- 3 cloves garlic, minced
- 2 cups coarsely chopped arugula, stems included
- 1/4 cup coarsely chopped fresh basil
- 1/2 cup olive oil
- 1/3 cup grated Parmesan cheese
- salt to taste
- 1 pinch cayenne pepper
- 1 (16 ounce) package dry pasta

Direction

- Combine the walnuts, garlic, arugula, and cilantro or basil in a food processor or blender. Whirl them just until they are coarsely chopped. While the machine is running, add the olive oil in a thin stream. Transfer the pesto to a bowl. (At this point the pesto can be frozen. Thaw it before proceeding.)
- Stir the Parmesan cheese, salt, and cayenne into the pesto
- Bring a large pot of salted water to a boil. Add the pasta, and cook it, stirring occasionally, until it is just tender. Drain the pasta, return it to the empty pot, and toss it with the pesto, adding a tablespoon or two of water if necessary to distribute the pesto evenly.

- Transfer the pasta to a serving bowl or to individual plates, garnish with additional Parmesan cheese and serve.

Nutrition Information

- Calories: 377 calories
- Total Fat: 19.6 g
- Cholesterol: 71 mg
- Sodium: 80 mg
- Total Carbohydrate: 40.5 g
- Protein: 10.5 g

156. Pasta with Asparagus and Lemon Sauce

"A quick midweek vegetarian pasta dish with asparagus and a creamy lemon sauce. I always use organic lemons whenever I use the zest."

Serving: 4 | Prep: 20 m | Cook: 20 m | Ready in: 40 m

Ingredients

- 2 lemons
- 1 (16 ounce) box penne pasta
- 5 tablespoons butter, divided
- 3/4 pound asparagus, trimmed and cut into 1-inch pieces
- salt and freshly ground black pepper to taste
- 3 tablespoons all-purpose flour
- 3/4 cup heavy cream
- 1 1/2 cups vegetable broth, or more to taste
- 4 sprigs fresh parsley, chopped
- 1 pinch white sugar, or to taste
- 2 ripe tomatoes, seeded and diced
- 1/2 cup freshly shaved Parmesan cheese

Direction

- Zest and juice 1 1/2 lemons. Cut remaining lemon half into wedges and set aside.
- Bring a large pot of lightly salted water to a boil. Add penne and cook, stirring occasionally, until tender yet firm to the bite, about 11 minutes. Drain, reserving 1 cup of cooking water.

- While penne is cooking, melt 2 tablespoons butter in a pot over medium heat and cook asparagus until softened, 4 to 5 minutes. Season with salt and pepper and remove from pot.
- Add remaining 3 tablespoons butter and heat until a pinch of flour sprinkled into the pot will just begin to bubble. Whisk in flour to form a thick paste the consistency of cake frosting. Continue cooking, whisking constantly, for about 5 minutes. Whisk in cream and vegetable broth and bring to a simmer. Simmer for 1 to 2 minutes.
- Stir lemon juice, lemon zest, and parsley into the sauce; season with salt, pepper, and sugar. Add asparagus and heat through, about 2 minutes. Add tomatoes and penne to the sauce and pour in some of the reserved cooking water. Serve with shaved Parmesan and lemon wedges.

Nutrition Information

- Calories: 811 calories
- Total Fat: 37.2 g
- Cholesterol: 108 mg
- Sodium: 512 mg
- Total Carbohydrate: 103.8 g
- Protein: 24.8 g

157. Pasta with Asparagus Goat Cheese and Lemon

"Asparagus, goat cheese, and lemon combine to make this lovely and simple spaghetti dish that I often make in the summer. It is super easy and ready in about 15 minutes, so it's a great recipe for dinner midweek or a fast weekend lunch."

Serving: 2 | Prep: 10 m | Cook: 20 m | Ready in: 30 m

Ingredients

- 1 (8 ounce) package spaghetti
- 1/2 pound asparagus, cut into bite-sized pieces
- 2 ounces chevre (soft goat cheese), crumbled
- 2 tablespoons olive oil
- 1 tablespoon chopped fresh basil, or more to taste
- 1/2 lemon, zested and juiced
- salt and ground black pepper to taste
- 2 tablespoons grated Parmesan cheese, or to taste (optional)

Direction

- Bring a large pot of lightly salted water to a boil. Cook spaghetti in the boiling water, stirring occasionally, for 9 minutes. Add asparagus to the pot. Continue cooking until spaghetti is tender yet firm to the bite, about 3 minutes. Drain spaghetti and asparagus, reserving some cooking water.
- Combine goat cheese, olive oil, basil, and lemon zest in a large bowl. Add hot spaghetti, asparagus, and 2 tablespoons of cooking water; mix well. Season with lemon juice, salt, and pepper. Serve with Parmesan cheese sprinkled on top.

Nutrition Information

- Calories: 688 calories
- Total Fat: 25.3 g
- Cholesterol: 27 mg
- Sodium: 310 mg
- Total Carbohydrate: 91.9 g
- Protein: 25.5 g

158. Pasta with Baby Broccoli and Beans

"Tuscan vegetarian comfort food. Omit the cheese to make it vegan."

Serving: 4 | Prep: 10 m | Cook: 15 m | Ready in: 25 m

Ingredients

- 1 (1 pound) package whole-wheat penne pasta
- 1/4 cup olive oil
- 1/2 whole head garlic, slivered
- 1/2 teaspoon crushed red pepper flakes
- 2 bunches baby broccoli (such as Broccolini®)
- 1 (14.5 ounce) can fava beans, rinsed and drained
- 1/4 cup sun-dried tomatoes
- 2 tablespoons grated Parmesan cheese

Direction

- Bring a large pot of lightly salted water to a boil. Cook the pasta in boiling water until cooked through yet firm to the bite, about 11 minutes; drain.
- While the pasta cooks, heat the olive oil in a skillet over medium heat. Cook the garlic and red pepper flakes in the hot oil briefly, about 1 minutes. Stir the broccolini into the garlic; cook and stir together for 5 minutes. Add the fava beans and sun-dried tomatoes and cook until the beans are completely warmed, 3 to 4 minutes. Remove from heat and toss with the drained pasta in a large bowl. Sprinkle with the Parmesan cheese to serve.

Nutrition Information

- Calories: 736 calories
- Total Fat: 16.8 g
- Cholesterol: 2 mg
- Sodium: 426 mg
- Total Carbohydrate: 113.4 g
- Protein: 35 g

159. Pasta with Cilantro Pesto and Barley

"This pasta dish is completely virtuous and completely delicious. And it's easy! Use any short, substantial pasta you like if you can't find orechietti. You can also make this with other fresh herbs. Good with more Parmesan on top!"

Serving: 4 | Prep: 15 m | Cook: 40 m | Ready in: 55 m

Ingredients

- 1 1/2 cups water
- 1/2 cup pearl barley
- 8 ounces uncooked orecchiette pasta
- 1 bunch cilantro
- 1/2 bunch green onions
- 1 cup grape tomatoes, halved
- 1/2 cup vegetable broth
- 1/4 cup Parmesan cheese
- 1 cup torn arugula leaves
- salt and pepper to taste

Direction

- In a saucepan, bring the 1 1/2 cups water to a boil. Stir in the barley. Reduce heat, cover, and simmer 30 minutes.
- Bring a large pot of lightly salted water to a boil. Add orecchiette pasta, and cook for 8 to 10 minutes or until al dente; drain.
- In a food processor, finely chop the cilantro, green onions, and 1/2 the tomatoes. Mix in the broth and Parmesan cheese, and process until well blended.

- In a large bowl, toss the barley, pasta, cilantro mixture, remaining tomatoes, and arugula. Season with salt and pepper, and serve immediately.

Nutrition Information

- Calories: 412 calories
- Total Fat: 3.6 g
- Cholesterol: 4 mg
- Sodium: 303 mg
- Total Carbohydrate: 81.6 g
- Protein: 14.2 g

160. Pasta with Fresh Tomato Sauce

"This pasta dish is wonderful served with a green salad. The best thing about it is that you can put this meal together in just a few minutes."

Serving: 8 | Prep: 15 m | Cook: 10 m | Ready in: 25 m

Ingredients

- 1 (16 ounce) package dry penne pasta
- 8 roma (plum) tomatoes, diced
- 1/2 cup Italian dressing
- 1/4 cup finely chopped fresh basil
- 1/4 cup diced red onion
- 1/4 cup grated Parmesan cheese

Direction

- Bring a large pot of lightly salted water to a boil. Place the penne pasta in the pot, cook 10 minutes, until al dente, and drain.
- Watch Now
- In a large bowl, toss the cooked pasta with the tomatoes, Italian dressing, basil, red onion, and Parmesan cheese.
- Watch Now

Nutrition Information

- Calories: 257 calories
- Total Fat: 3.1 g

- Cholesterol: 3 mg
- Sodium: 248 mg
- Total Carbohydrate: 46.9 g
- Protein: 9.8 g

Printed in Great Britain
by Amazon